KB197477

안녕? 한글!

ANNYEONG? HANGEUL!

First published in 2024 by Hello Korean Inc.

Published by Hur. Dae woo
Marketing by Park. Sang ho
Designed by Brunch Park
Cover Image by Lee. Jung jin
Character Design by Lee. Chae min

ISBN 979-11-988638-0-5 93700
eBook ISBN 979-11-988638-1-2 15700

Printed and bound in Republic of Korea by Hello Printec

Prof. Jieun Kiaer

with Derek Driggs and Hyung-Suk Kim

Hello Korean

Welcome to learning Hangeul, the Korean alphabet! This book is for anyone who loves K-pop, K-dramas, Korean food, or wants to travel to Korea. It's also perfect if you just want to study the Korean alphabet. We hope you enjoy discovering how to read and write Hangeul with fun activities and interesting words.

We aim to make learning Hangeul enjoyable and accessible, even if you're a complete beginner. Through this book, you'll not only learn to read and write Hangeul but also discover many interesting Korean words and phrases.

Each chapter is packed with K-culture words to enhance your learning experience. Plus, every page features a QR code that links to audio instructions in multiple languages, including Indonesian, Chinese, Japanese, French, and, of course, Korean (more languages will be added). These recordings will guide you through the pronunciation of Korean words from left to right and top to bottom, with numbered guides for ease of use. This unique book allows friends from around the world to learn the Korean alphabet in their own languages. So, are you ready to start this exciting journey? Let's dive in and explore the beautiful world of Hangeul together!

About Us

This book is part of the *Annyeong Korean Textbook* series, which aims to spread the Korean language worldwide in many languages, not just English. For the first time, we are providing instructions in multiple languages to reach learners all around the globe. In this series, we have characters who are learning Korean. Let us introduce them to you!

Sarang

shares a flat in Seoul Villa and is the leader of room 101 on the first floor, which has four rooms. When new people arrive, she explains the flat rules. Sarang was born in the UK to a Korean mother and a British father. She spoke Korean well as a child but forgot much of it after living in the UK. She is now back in Korea for a year to study the language and works part-time at the shared apartment.

Priya

is very interested in Korean culture because of K-pop. She hopes to work and live in Korea in the future. Priya does not eat pork.

Haru

is from Japan and became interested in Korea through Korean dramas. She studies art and has enrolled in a language school to learn Korean. Haru cannot eat spicy food well.

Professor Caroline,

or Caroline Ssaem (Teacher), teaches history at a university in the United States. She is fascinated by Korean history and decided to come to Korea for a month after reading Korean novels.

Jina Ssaem

is your cheerful Korean teacher in Annyeong Korean.
She's passionate about languages and loves to cook!
With her, you'll learn Korean and maybe even taste some yummy Korean snacks.
Jina-Ssaem makes every lesson feel like a fun adventure!

Sophia

is from France and is an Olympic butterfly swimmer. She enjoys swimming in the Han River.

Yu Tao

is the leader of room 201 on the second floor. He is from China, a mathematics genius, and enjoys playing baduk (a Korean strategy board game) and e-sports.

Sam

is from Australia and dreams of becoming a chef. He loves playing football and baseball and often goes to baseball games.

Gabriel

is from Canada. His grandfather, a war veteran, inspired his interest in Korea. Gabriel studies architecture and is very interested in hanoks (Korean traditional houses).

CHARACTER INTRODUCTIONS

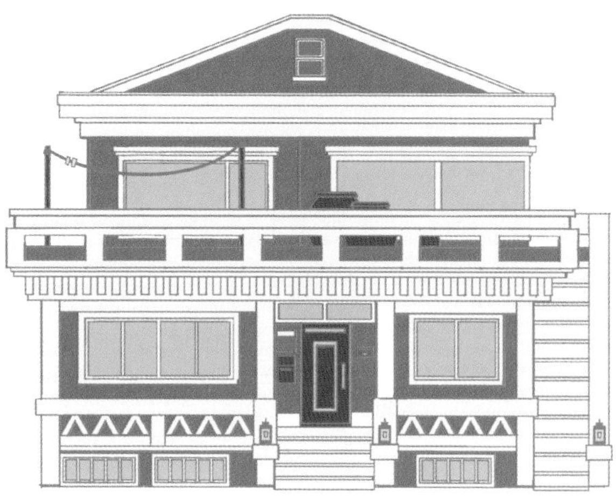

Sarang's Villa

Table of Contents

Chapter 01

Warm Up with the Ganada Song

Before we dive into learning Hangul-the Korean alphabets, let's start with a K-pop song called "Ganada Song" designed for you!

This song is similar to the ABC song. They attach the vowel "a" to consonants and sing "Ga, Na, Da, Ra, Ma, Ba, Sa, A, Ja, Cha, Ka, Ta, Pa, Ha"!

Shall we try? Sing along!

Ga, Na, Da, Ra, Ma, Ba, Sa, A, Ja, Cha, Ka, Ta, Pa, Ha.

가나다라마바사아자차카타파하

Now, let's listen to the Ga, Na, Da song.

Ganada Song

After listening to the song several times, try to sing along with the help of the romanized letters!

가 나 다 라 마 바 사 아 자 차 카 타 파 하

[ga na da ra ma ba sa a ja cha ka ta pa ha]

빠 람 빠 람 Let's sing along

[ppa ram ppa ram Let's sing along]

가 나 다 라 마 바 사 아 자 차 카 타 파 하

[ga na da ra ma ba sa a ja cha ka ta pa ha]

빠 람 빠 람 singing together

[ppa ram ppa ram singing together]

Let's walk and sing / Let's hold hands together

아 야 어 여 오 요 우 유 으 이

[a ya eo yeo o yo u yu eu i]

가.슴 을 펴 고

[ga. seum eul pyeo go]

나.를 따 라 해 봐

[na. reul tta ra hae bwa]

다.함 께

[da. ham kke]

라.라 라

[ra. ra ra]

마.음 열 고

[ma. eum yeol go]

바.라 봐
[ba. ra bwa]

사.이 좋 게
[sa. i jok ge]

아.름 답 게 Oh~
[a. reum dap ge Oh~]

자. 따 라 해 봐
[ja. tta ra hae bwa]

차. 렷. 하 나 둘 셋
[cha. ryeot ha na dul set]

카.네 이 션
[ka. ne i syeon]

타.고 서
[ta. go seo]

파.란 하 늘
[pa. ran ha neul]

보 고 웃 어 봐
[bo go us eo bwa]

하 하 하 하
[ha ha ha ha]

하! 하! 하!
[ha! ha! ha!]

가 나 다 라 마 바 사 아 자 차 카 타 파 하
[ga na da ra ma ba sa a ja cha ka ta pa ha]

빠 람 빠 람 Let's sing along
[ppa ram ppa ram Let's sing along]

가 나 다 라 마 바 사 아 자 차 카 타 파 하
[ga na da ra ma ba sa a ja cha ka ta pa ha]

빠 람 빠 람 singing together
[ppa ram ppa ram singing together]

Let's walk and sing / Let's hold hands together

아 야 어 여 오 요 우 유 으 이
[a ya eo yeo o yo u yu eu i]

We're together / Together is better / Me and You, we're one
Melodies are shared like a dream! / Languages Our look, Oh!
All isn't the same / Many differences
Let's sing me and you / Melody makes us one, together!
Singing brings peace and love

가 나 다 라 마 바 사 아 자 차 카 타 파 하
[ga na da ra ma ba sa a ja cha ka ta pa ha]

우 리 에 게 꿈 을 주 는 글
[u ri e ge kkum eul ju neun geul]

가 나 다 라 마 바 사 아 자 차 카 타 파 하
[ga na da ra ma ba sa a ja cha ka ta pa ha]

Born to give us hope and the dream

Let's walk and sing / Let's hold hands together

아 야 어 여 오 요 우 유 으 이
[a ya eo yeo o yo u yu eu i]

Let's go!

With this K-pop song, are you ready to embark on your journey with Hangeul?

Let's go!

Chapter 02

What is Hangeul?

Now, you are going to read a conversation between your friends. Make sure to remember the information shared by the Jina Ssaem (쌤, teacher). You'll need to take a mini quiz at the end of your learning—see if you can get baek-jeom-man-jeom (백점만점)—full marks!

Sarang

Hello! Annyeonghaseyo! I have been dreaming of moving to Korea for years, and I'm finally going! My first step is to learn to read Korean. Join me and my friends as we learn about Hangeul!

Jina Ssaem

Annyeonghaseyo! I'll do my best to help you along the way! I'm excited for your Korean journey to start.

Sarang

So, **WHAT** is Hangeul?

Jina Ssaem

Hangeul(한글) is the Korean phonetic alphabet.
You can mix and match these characters to make up to 11,172 unique syllables, all of which can be easily sounded out.
When Hangeul was created, it was said that you can learn it in anywhere from one morning to 10 days, even if you're not a genius.
Hangeul is simple and logical, making it quick and easy to pick up.

Priya

Okay, so **WHO** made Hangeul?

Jina Ssaem

King Sejong(세종 대왕) was a brilliant king in Korean history.
With help from a team of scholars, he personally created Hangeul.
King Sejong wrote about making Hangeul.
Here's a simple version of what he said:

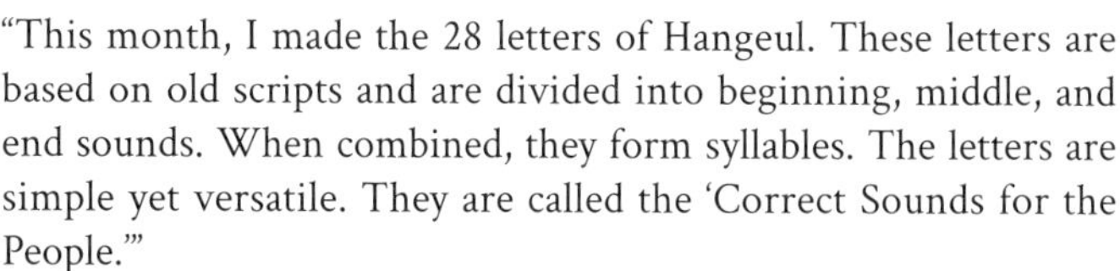

"This month, I made the 28 letters of Hangeul. These letters are based on old scripts and are divided into beginning, middle, and end sounds. When combined, they form syllables. The letters are simple yet versatile. They are called the 'Correct Sounds for the People.'"

King Sejong wanted a writing system that was easy for everyone to learn, so more people could read and write in Korean.

Haru

WHEN did King Sejong create Hangeul?

Jina Ssaem

The Korean language as it's spoken today has been around for thousands of years. But Hangeul was completed in late December of 1443 and officially promulgated by King Sejong in 1446. It is one of the youngest writing systems in the world!

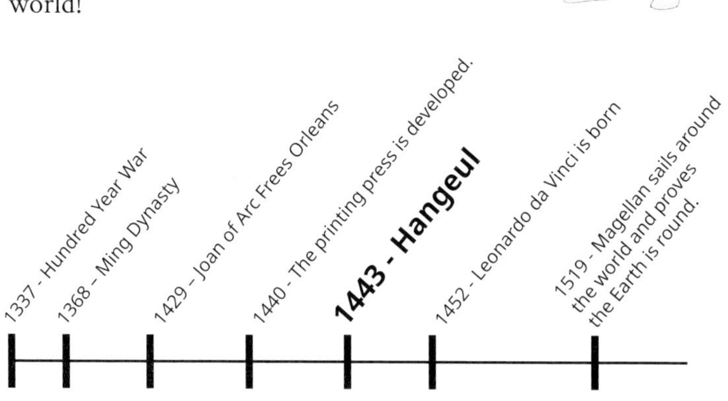
1337 - Hundred Year War
1368 – Ming Dynasty
1429 – Joan of Arc Frees Orleans
1440 - The printing press is developed.
1443 - Hangeul
1452 - Leonardo da Vinci is born
1519 - Magellan sails around the world and proves the Earth is round.

Yu Tao

WHERE did Hangeul come from?

Jina Ssaem

King Sejong was an early king in the Joseon Dynasty, which is the older name for modern day Korea. Hangeul is totally native to Korea

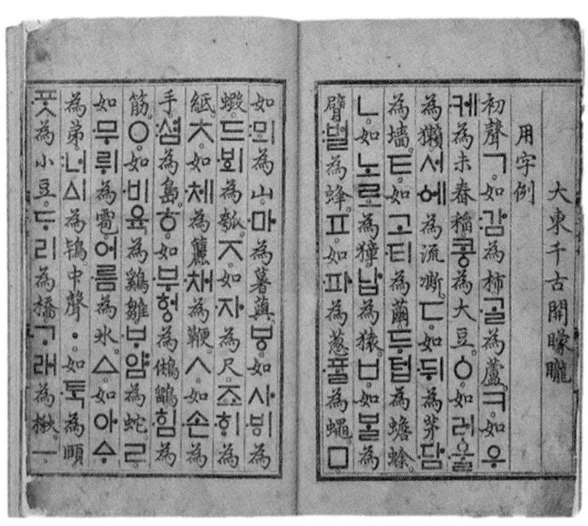

大東千古開曚矓

用字例

初聲ㄱ。如감爲柿。ᄀᆞᆯ爲蘆。ㅋ。如우케爲未舂稻。콩爲大豆。ㆁ。如러ᇰ爲獺。서에爲流凘。ㄷ。如뒤爲茅。담爲墻。ㅌ。如고티爲繭。두텁爲蟾蜍。ㄴ。如노로爲獐。납爲猿。ㅂ。如ᄇᆞᆯ爲臂。벌爲蜂。ㅍ。如파爲葱。ᄑᆞᆯ爲蠅。ㅁ。如뫼爲山。마爲薯藇。ㅸ。如사ᄫᅵ爲蝦。드ᄫᅴ爲瓠。ㅈ。如자爲尺。죠ᄒᆡ爲紙。ㅊ。如체爲籭。채爲鞭。ㅅ。如손爲手。셤爲島。ㅎ。如부헝爲鵂鶹。힘爲筋。ㅇ。如비육爲鷄雛。ᄇᆞ얌爲蛇。ㄹ。如무뤼爲雹。어름爲氷。ㅿ。如아ᅀᆞ爲弟。너ᅀᅵ爲鴇。中聲ㆍ。如톡爲頥。ᄑᆞᆺ爲小豆。ᄃᆞ리爲橋。ᄀᆞ래爲楸。ㅡ

Hunminjeongeum Haeryebon

Sam

Okay, but if the Korean language has been around so long, **WHY** was Hangeul introduced?

Jina Ssaem

Before Hangeul was created, Korean people had to use Chinese characters to write things down. King Sejong himself wrote:

"The Korean language is different from Chinese, so it is hard to express Korean by using Chinese characters. Hence, many people having something to put into words are unable to express their feelings. To overcome such distressing circumstances, I have newly devised twenty-eight letters that everyone can learn with ease and use with convenience in daily life."

The King's choice to help illiterate people, like women and lower classes, was not popular. Some nobles and powerful figures thought Korea should be trying to be more like China, and that lower classes didn't need literacy.

Despite opposition, Hangeul flourished among ordinary people, fulfilling King Sejong's vision of a simple, easy-to-learn writing system for everyone.

Sofia

I've never heard of someone inventing an alphabet! **HOW** did Sejong do that?

Jina Ssaem

King Sejong used advanced linguistic principles to design the shapes of his letters. Consonants were modeled after the shape the mouth makes in their production, and vowels were modeled after Daoist spiritual principles.

In the following, you can see how the different letters fit the shape the mouth makes when making their sounds! You can also see the Daoist meanings of the basic vowel shapes (Heaven, Earth, and Human).

ㄱ

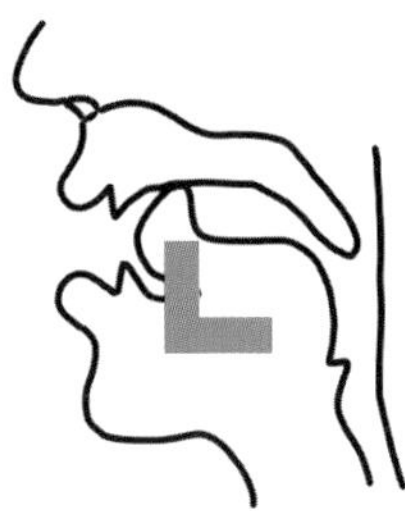
ㄴ

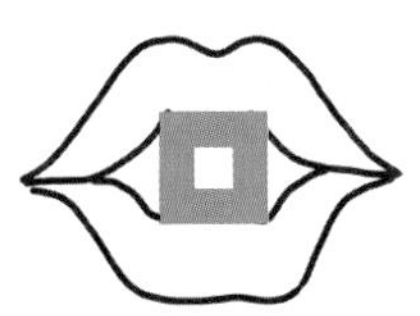
ㅁ

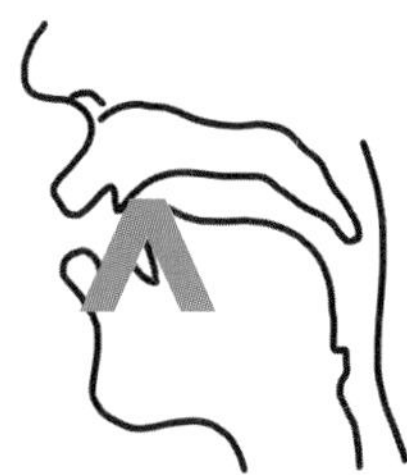
ㅅ

ㅇ

Heaven
Earth
Human

Sarang

Now that we've learned about Hangeul, I guess it's time to start learning!

Jina Ssaem

Take a deep breath and take your time. You'll get this in no time!

Mini Quiz Your Path to Becoming a K-pop Idol through Hangeul!

Part 1. Fill in the Blanks

Complete the sentences using the correct information from the conversation. Choose the correct answer from the options provided.

1. Hangeul is the Korean _______ alphabet.
   a) symbolic b) phonetic c) numerical
2. Hangeul was created by _______ with help from a team of scholars.
   a) King Sejong b) Prince Yeonsan c) Queen Seondeok
3. Before Hangeul, Korean people used _______ characters to write things down.
   a) Japanese b) Mongolian c) Chinese
4. The design of Hangeul letters is based on _______ principles.
   a) mathematical b) linguistic c) artistic

Part 2. Matching

Match the information with the correct description. Draw lines to connect each term with its correct description.

1. Hangeul •	• a) Creator of Hangeul
2. King Sejong •	• b) The year Hangeul was completed
3. 1443 •	• c) Where Hangeul originated
4. Joseon Dynasty •	• d) The Korean phonetic alphabet
5. Chinese characters •	• e) Used by Koreans before Hangeul was created

ANSWERS

Part 1. b a c b *Part 2.* 1-d; 2-a; 3-b; 4-c; 5-e

Chapter 03

Hangeul in Romanized Letters

First, let's talk about *romanized letters*-the way that Korean sounds are written in English letters.

Why is this important?

Romanized letters help you understand how to pronounce Korean words even if you can't read Hangul yet. These are the official romanized letters used by the Korean government, so you will see them in names, places, and roman Korean words.
Sometimes, the way Korean words are spelled using English letters might seem a bit confusing or counterintuitive. Don't worry, you'll get the hang of it with practice!

BASIC VOWELS

Now, let's look at the vowels. We will list the Korean characters and their romanized spelling. Refer back to the romanization chart if you need to review the pronunciation. Colour coding information: red is for heart on your side, blue is running underneath, purple is a mix of red and blue because it uses both ways, and green for consonants.

VOWEL	ROMANIZATION
ㅏ	*a*
ㅓ	*eo*
ㅗ	*o*
ㅜ	*u*
ㅡ	*eu*
ㅣ	*i*

아

Romanized Letter a

Hangeul ㅏ

English sound
ah as in f***a***ther or b***a***rk

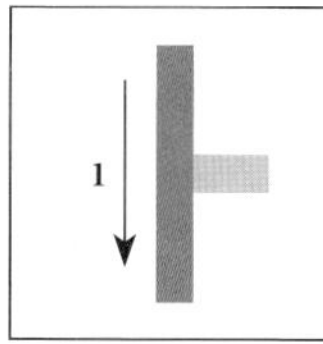

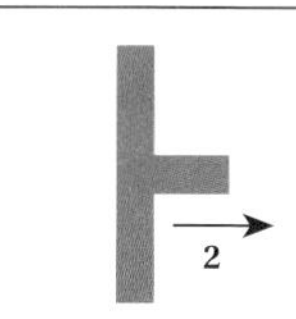

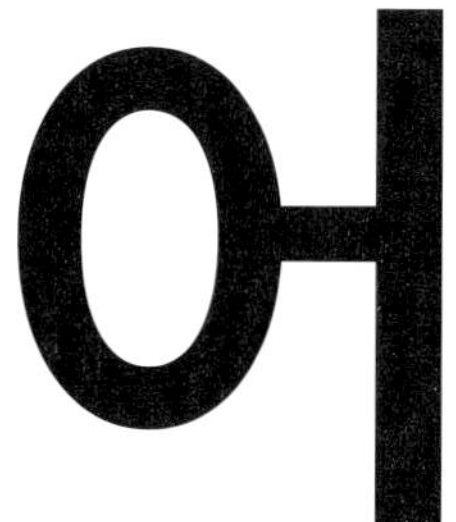

Romanized Letter eo

Hangeul ㅓ

English sound
uh as in f***u***n or s***o***n,
with more rounded lips

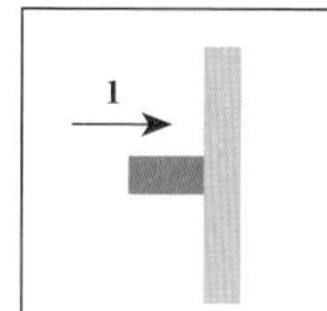

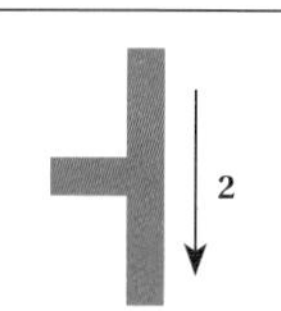

Romanized Letter o

Hangeul ㅗ

English sound
oh as in l**o**w or t***oe***

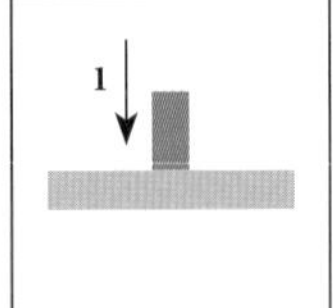

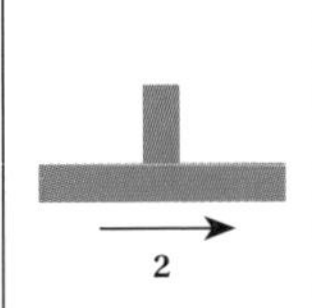

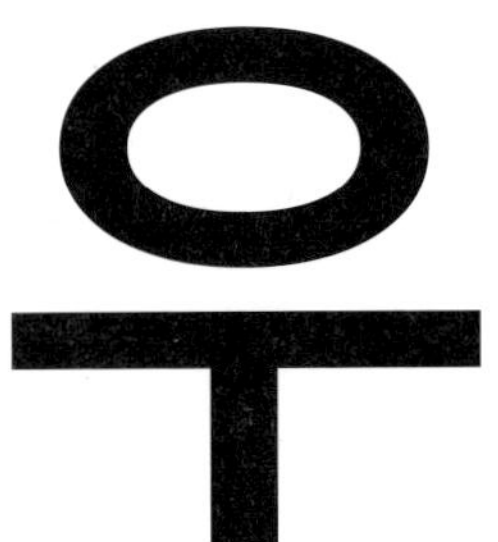

Romanized Letter u

Hangeul ㅜ

English sound
oo as in bl***ue*** or t***oo***

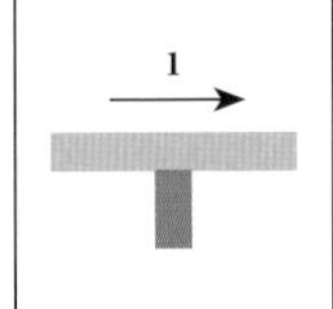

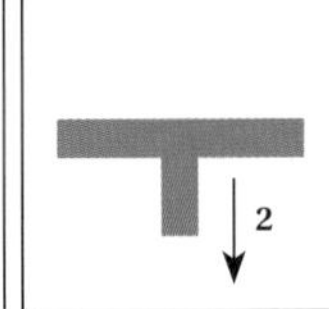

으

Romanized Letter eu

Hangeul ㅡ

English sound
eu as in f***oo***t or p***u***t

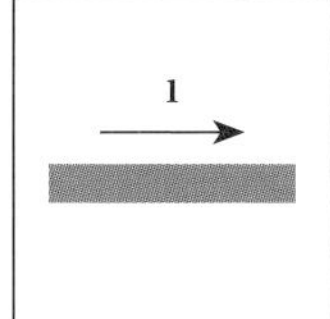

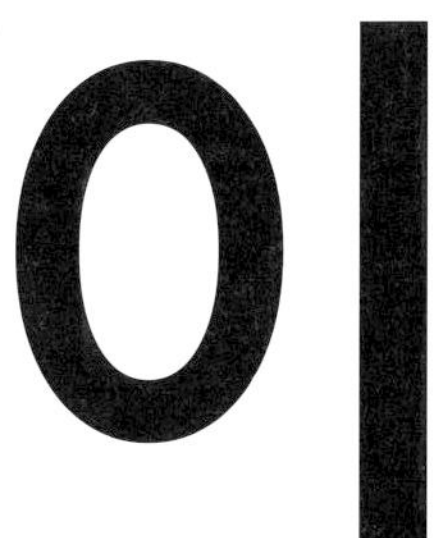

Romanized Letter i

Hangeul ㅣ

English sound
ee as in s***ee*** or m***e***

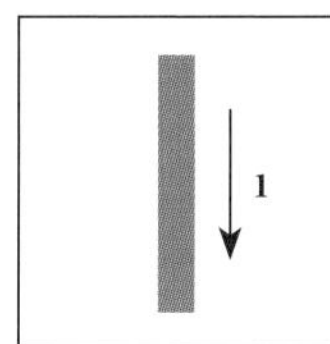

COMPLEX VOWELS

In addition to the simple vowel sounds we've already practiced, there are also more complex vowel sounds.
The first set of these complex vowel sounds are based on the basic vowels we have already learned. To make these vowels, we simply add a line (ㅡ) (ㅣ) to a basic vowel, which changes the vowel to start with a "y" sound.

VOWEL	ROMANIZATION
ㅑ	*ya*
ㅕ	*yeo*
ㅛ	*yo*
ㅠ	*yu*
ㅒ	*ye*
ㅖ	*ye*

야

Romanized Letter ya

Hangeul ㅑ

English sound
ya as in ***ya***rd

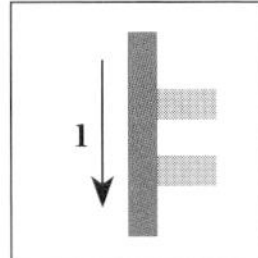

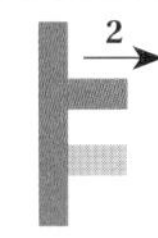

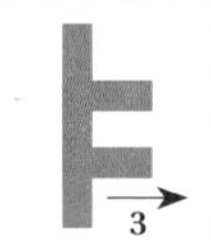

Romanized Letter yeo

Hangeul ㅕ

English sound
yuh as in ***you***ng

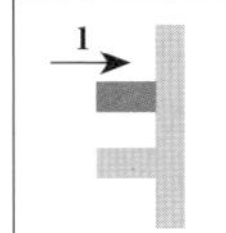

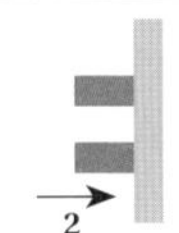

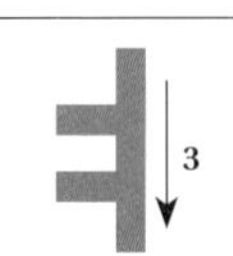

Romanized Letter yo

Hangeul ㅛ

English sound

yo as in ***yo**gurt*
(American pronunciation)

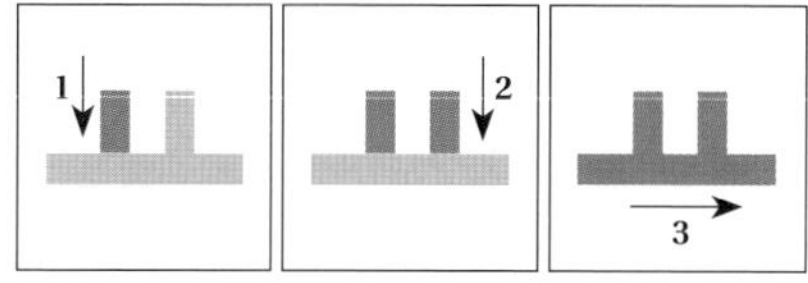

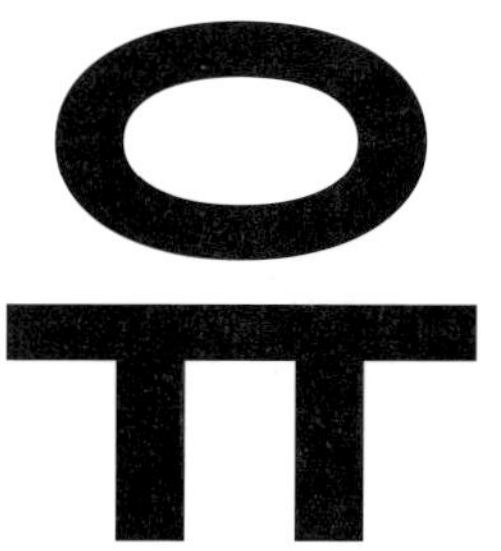

Romanized Letter yu

Hangeul ㅠ

English sound

yoo as in ***you***

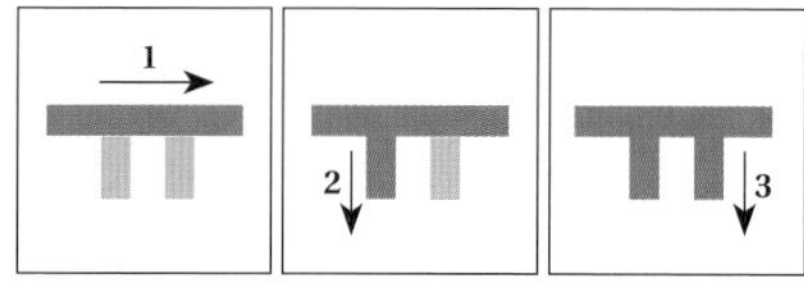

얘

Romanized Letter yae

Hangeul ㅒ

English sound
yeh as in ***ya***y

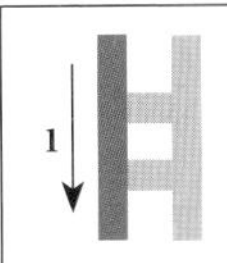

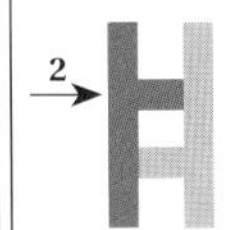

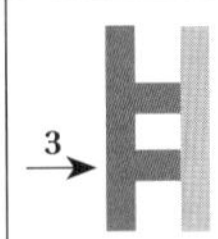

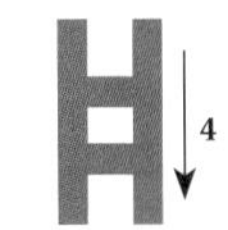

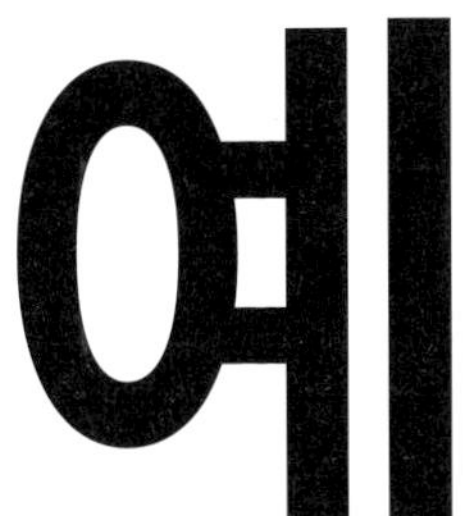

Romanized Letter ye

Hangeul ㅖ

English sound
yeh as in ***ya***y

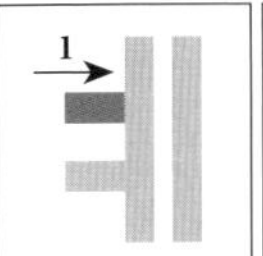

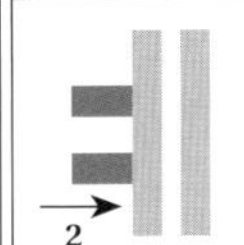

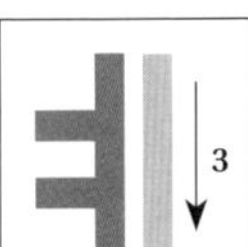

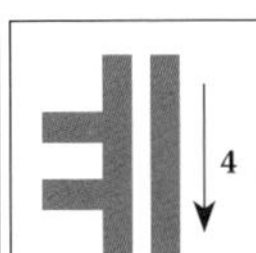

Try to write the following words:

ㅑ

야구 *Baseball* .... [yagu]

야채 *Vegetable* .... [yachae]

ㅕ

여자 *Woman* .... [yeoja]

여권 *Passport* .... [yeogwon]

ㅛ

요리 *Cooking* .... [yori]

요거트 *Yogurt* .... [yogeoteu]

ㅠ

유리 *Glass* .... [yuri]

유자차 *Citron tea* .... [yujacha]

ㅒ

얘기책 *Storybook* .... [yaegichaek]

얘들아 *Hey kids* .... [yaedeura]

ㅖ

예쁘다 *Pretty* .... [yeppeuda]

예약 *Reservation* .... [yeyak]

The next set of complex vowels are *diphthongs,* which means they are made by combining two other vowel sounds.

COMBINATION	DIPHTHONG	ROMANIZATION
ㅏ + ㅣ	ㅐ	*ae*
ㅓ + ㅣ	ㅔ	*e*
ㅗ + ㅏ	ㅘ	*wa*
ㅗ + ㅐ	ㅙ	*wae*
ㅗ + ㅣ	ㅚ	*oe*
ㅜ + ㅓ	ㅝ	*wo*
ㅜ + ㅔ	ㅞ	*we*
ㅜ + ㅣ	ㅟ	*wi*
ㅡ + ㅣ	ㅢ	*ui*

애

Romanized Letter ae

Hangeul ㅐ

English sound
eh as in t***a***ke or ch***a***se

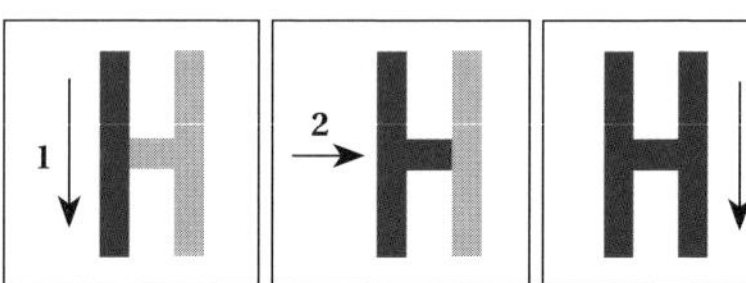

Romanized Letter e

Hangeul ㅔ

English sound
eh as in b***e***d or d***ea***d

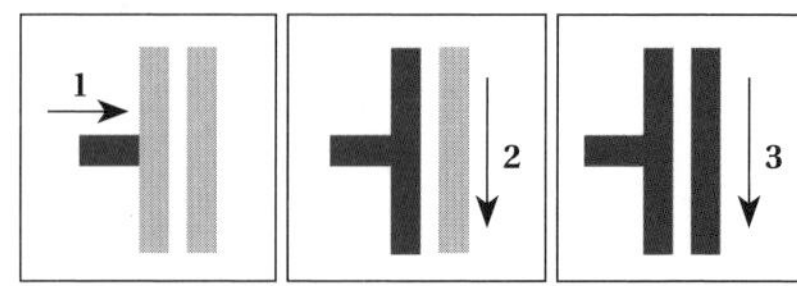

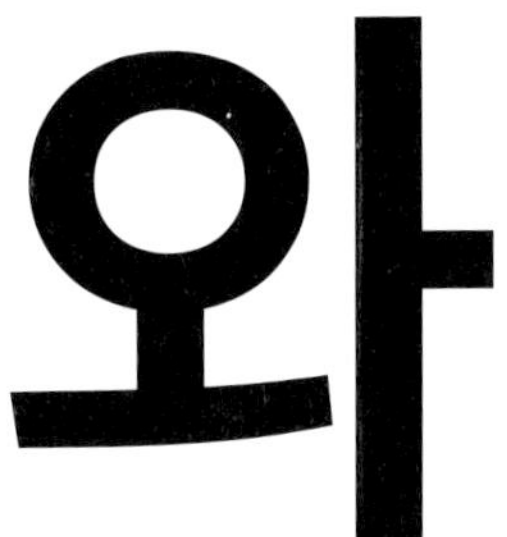

Romanized Letter wa

Hangeul ㅘ

English sound
wah as in ***wi**se*

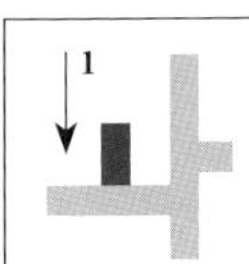

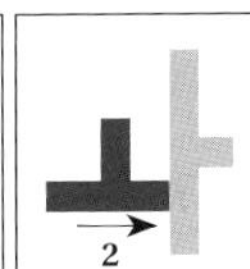

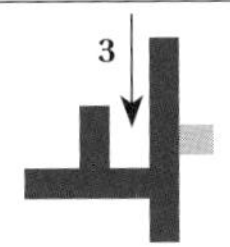

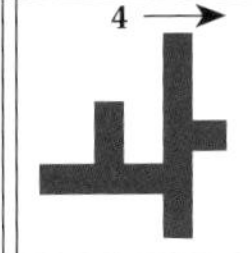

Romanized Letter wae

Hangeul ㅙ

English sound
weh as in ***wa**it* or ***we**ight*

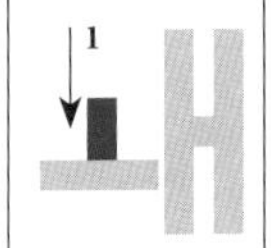

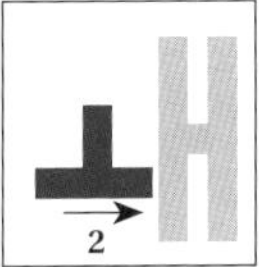

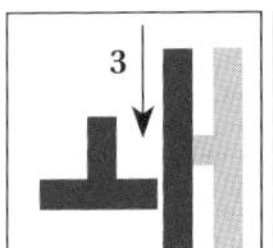

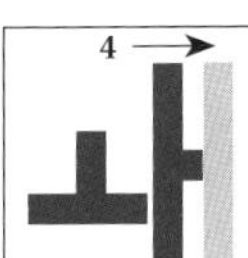

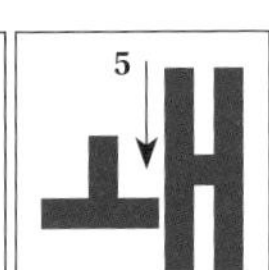

외

Romanized Letter oe

Hangeul ㅚ

English sound
weh as in ***wa***it or ***we***ight

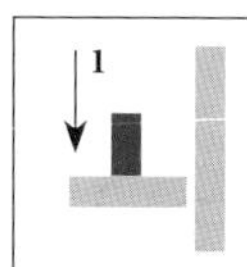

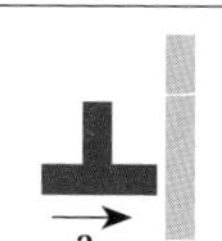

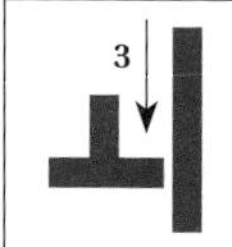

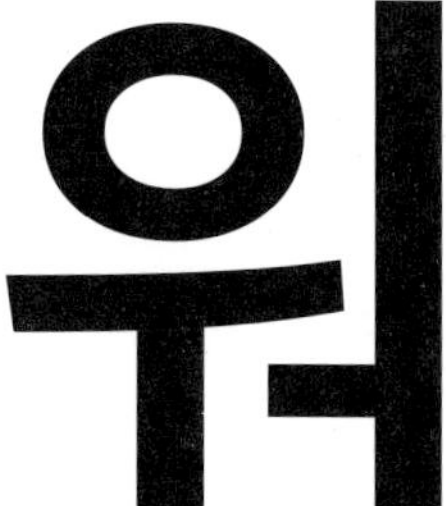

Romanized Letter wo

Hangeul ㅝ

English sound
wo as in ***wa***llet

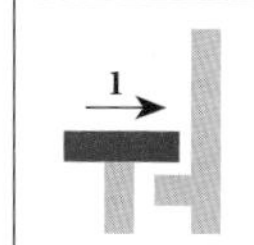

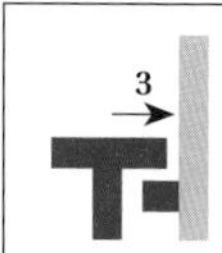

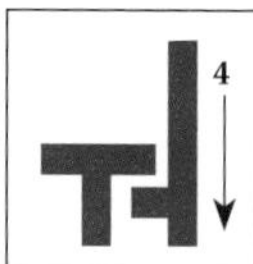

Romanized Letter we

Hangeul ㅞ

English sound
weh as in ***wa***it or ***we***ight

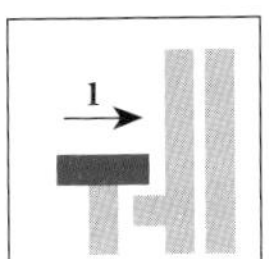

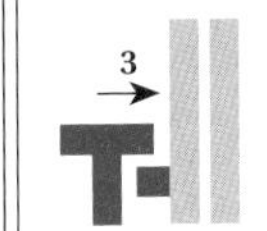

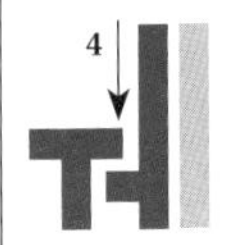

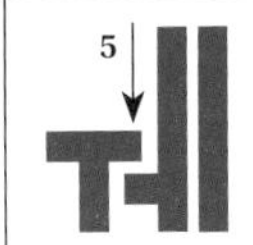

Romanized Letter wi

Hangeul ㅟ

English sound
we as in ***wea***ve or ***wee***d

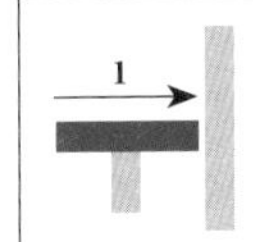

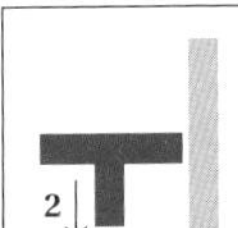

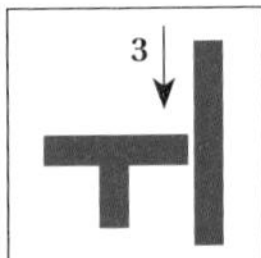

Romanized Letter ui

Hangeul ㅢ

English sound
a combination of *eu* and *i* above

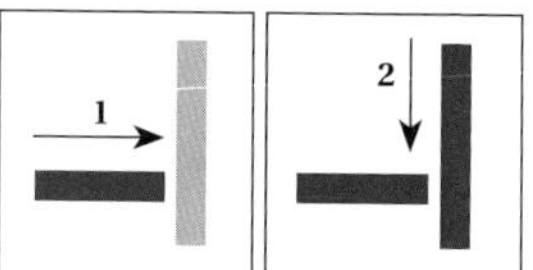

Try to write the following words:

ㅐ

개미 *Ant* .... [gaemi]

사랑해 *I love you* .... [saranghae]

ㅔ

메뉴 *Menu* .... [menyu]

케이크 *Cake* .... [keikeu]

ㅘ

과일 *Fruit* .... [gwail]

과자 *Snack* .... [gwaja]

ㅙ

왜 *Why* .... [wae]

돼지 *Pig* .... [dwaeji]

ㅚ

외국 *Foreign country* .... [oeguk]

회사 *Company* .... [hoesa]

ㅝ

원하다 *To want* .... [wonhada]

원숭이 *Monkey* .... [wonsungi]

ㅞ
웨이터 Waiter [weiteo]
웹사이트 Website [wepsaiteu]
ㅟ
위험 Danger [wiheom]
위 Up/Above [wi]
ㅢ
의사 Doctor [uisa]
의자 Chair [uija]

Just like the basic vowels we already covered, each of these vowels combines with various consonants to create different syllable sounds. Below are some examples of those combinations.

뱌	***bya***	뮈	***mwi***
겨	***gyeo***	붜	***bwo***
료	***ryo***	갸	***gya***
뮤	***myu***	뢔	***rwae***
대	***dae***	뇨	***nyo***

얘	***yae***	**새**	***sae***
네	***ne***	**퉤**	***dwe***
혜	***hye***	**유**	***yu***
콰	***kwa***	**죠**	***jyo***
푀	***poe***	**혀**	***hyeo***
쇄	***swae***	**냬**	***nyae***
퉈	***two***	**킈**	***kui***
줴	***jwe***	**체**	***che***

Try To Write The Following Words:

비행기 *Airplane* .... [bihaenggi]

겨울 *Winter* .... [gyeoul]

뮤지컬 *Musical* .... [myujikeol]

돼지 *Pig* .... [dwaeji]

사랑해 *I love you* .... [saranghae]

유자차 *Citron tea* .... [yujacha]

BASIC CONSONANTS

Romanized Letter g

Hangeul ㄱ

English sound
a softer version (unvoiced) of *g* as in ***g***ood

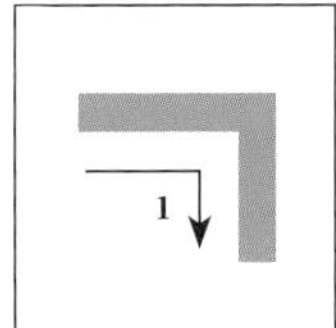

Romanized Letter n

Hangeul ㄴ

English sound
n as in ***n***ame

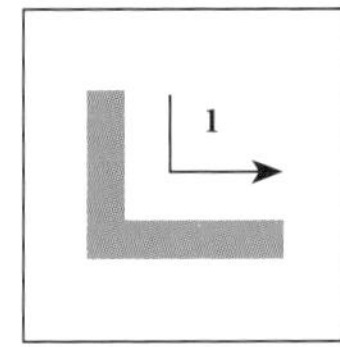

Romanized Letter d

Hangeul ㄷ

English sound
a softer version (unvoiced) of *d* as in ***d***awn

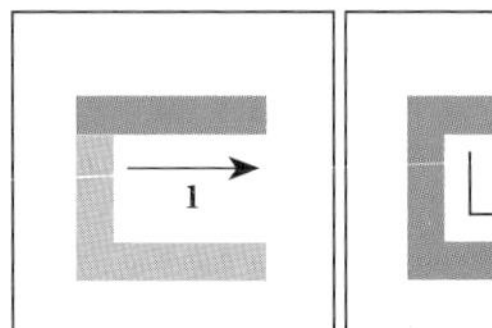

Romanized Letter r

Hangeul ㄹ

English sound
a *r* that involves rolling and vibrating the tongue

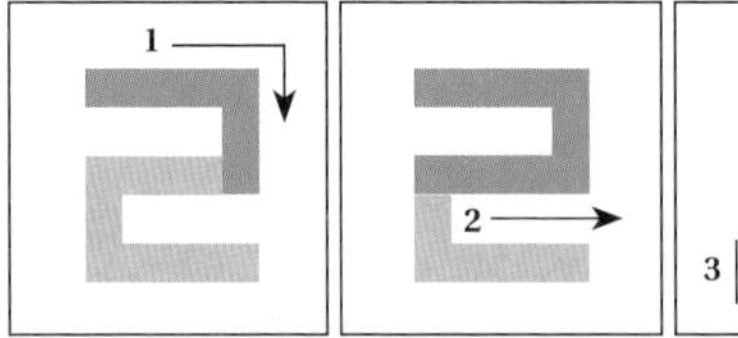

Romanized Letter m

Hangeul ㅁ

English sound
m as in ***m***ask

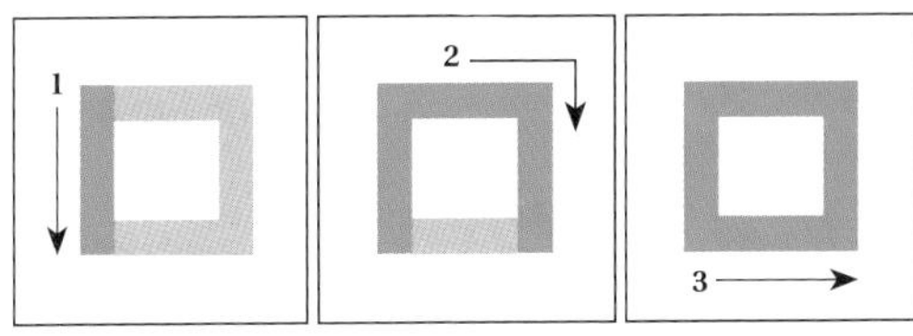

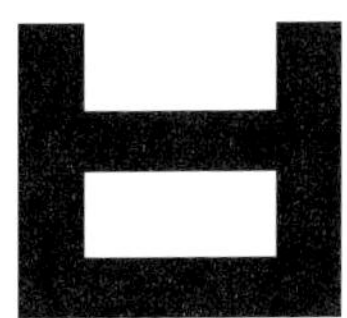

Romanized Letter b

Hangeul ㅂ

English sound
a softer version (unvoiced) of *b* as in ***b***all

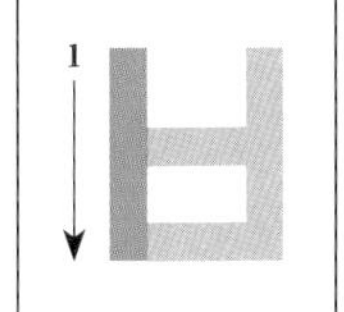

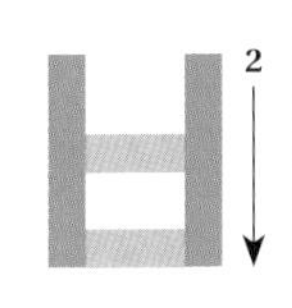

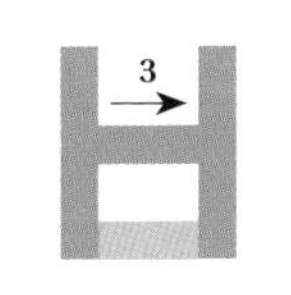

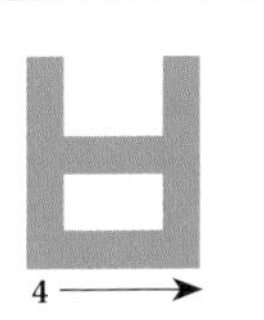

Romanized Letter S

Hangeul ㅅ

English sound

s as in ***s**ad*

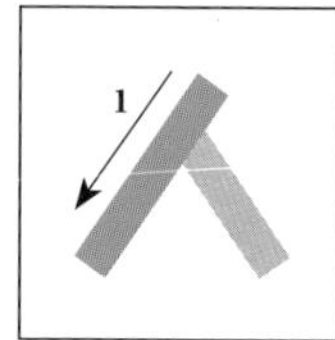

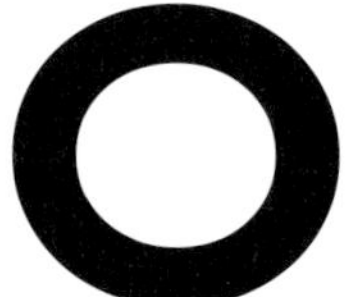

Romanized Letter ng

Hangeul ㅇ

English sound

ng as in so***ng***
(at the end of a word)

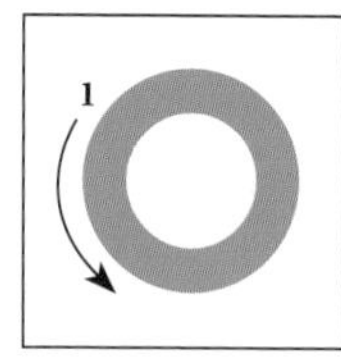

Romanized Letter j

Hangeul ㅈ

English sound
a softer version (unvoiced) of *j* as in ***j***et

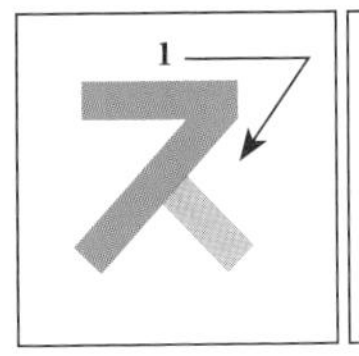

ASPIRATED CONSONANTS

Romanized Letter ch

Hangeul ㅊ

English sound
ch as in ***ch***art

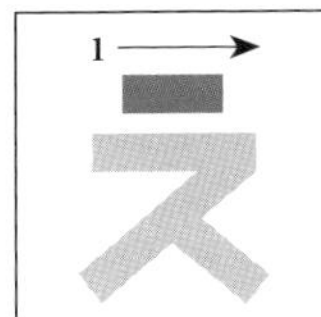

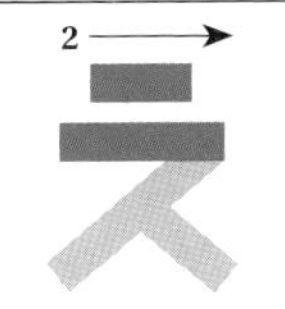

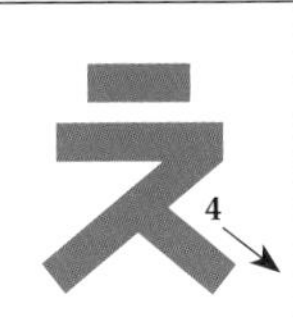

Romanized Letter k

Hangeul ㅋ

English sound
k as in ***k***id

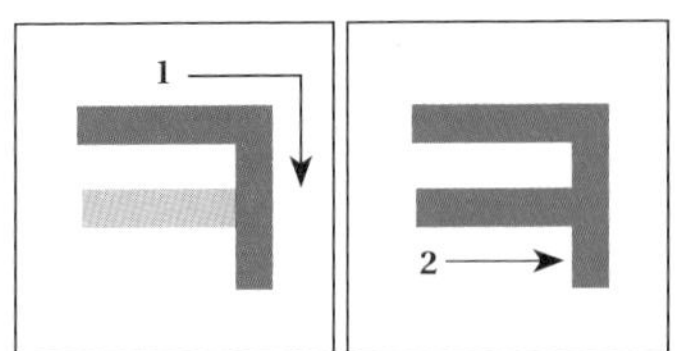

Romanized Letter t

Hangeul ㅌ

English sound

t as in ***t***all

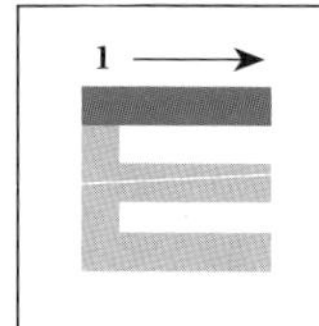

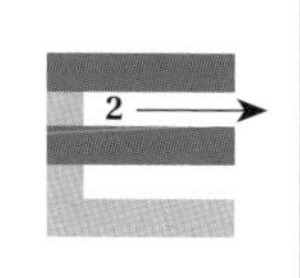

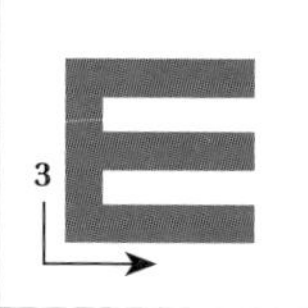

Romanized Letter p

Hangeul ㅍ

English sound

p as in ***p***aper

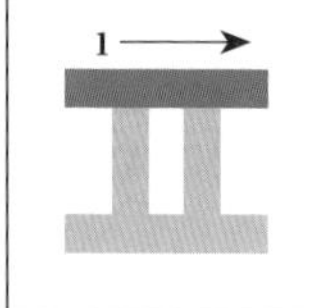

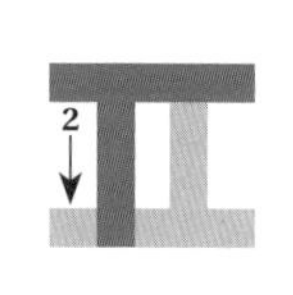

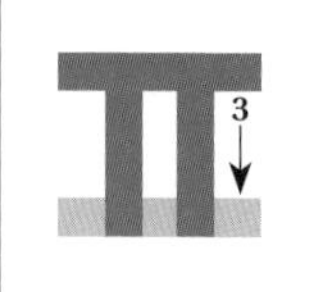

Romanized Letter h

Hangeul ㅎ

English sound
h as in ***h***ow or ***h***ot

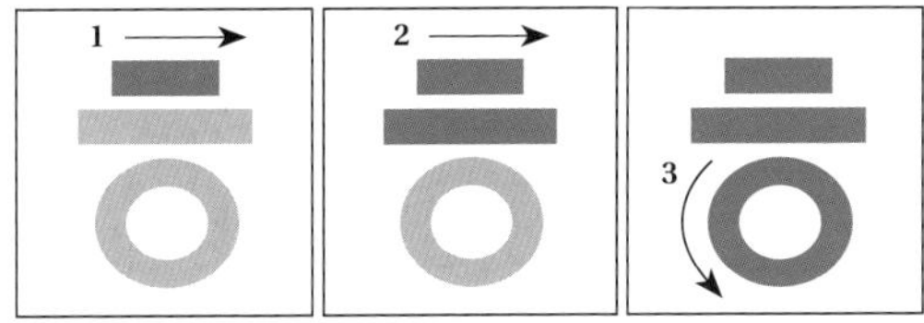

REINFORCED CONSONANTS

In addition to these aspirated consonants, Korean also has several *reinforced* consonants. These are formed by doubling other consonant sounds by closing up the throat, to make a harder, more forceful sound.

Romanized Letter kk

Hangeul ㄲ

English sound

a tenser *g* than
the *g* in ***g***ood

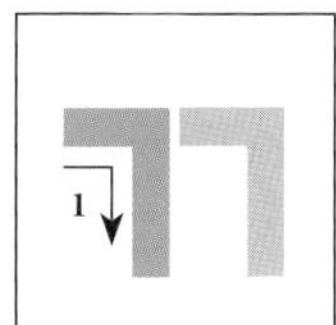

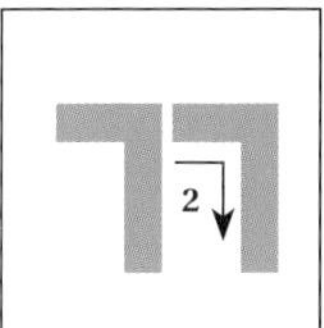

Romanized Letter tt

Hangeul ㄸ

English sound

a tenser *d* than
the *d* in ***d***og

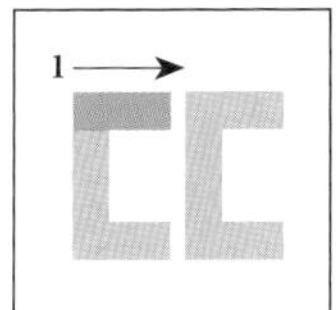

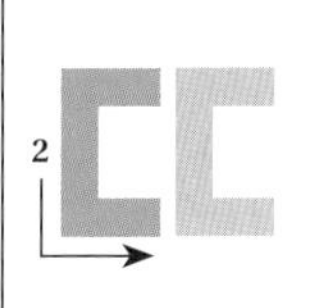

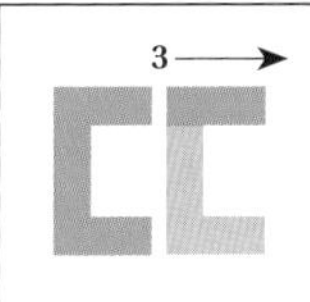

Romanized Letter pp

Hangeul ㅃ

English sound
a tenser *b* than the *b* in ***b**all*

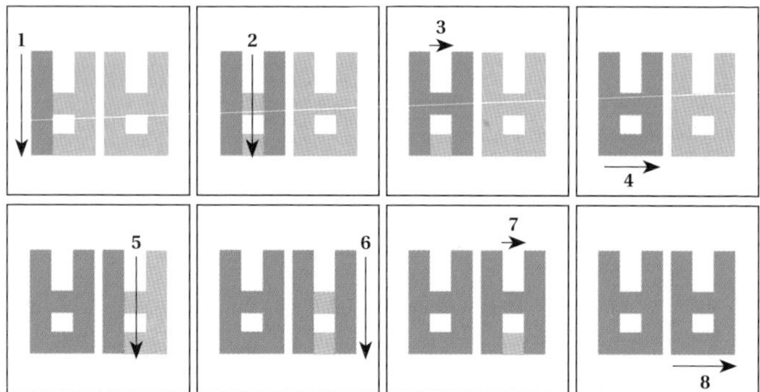

Romanized Letter ss

Hangeul ㅆ

English sound
a tenser *s* than the *s* in ***s**ad*

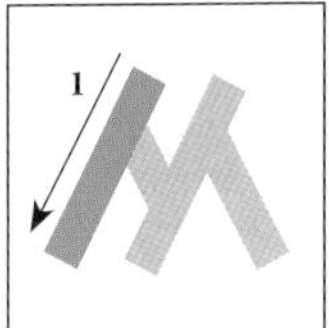

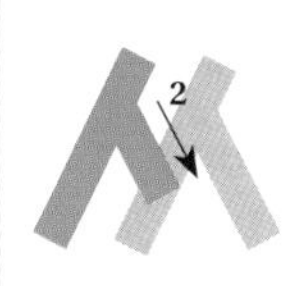

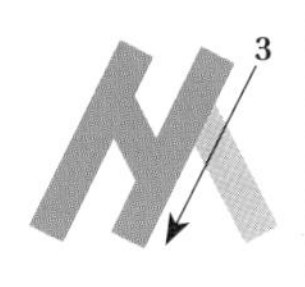

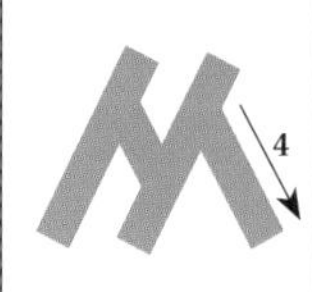

Romanized Letter jj

Hangeul ㅉ

English sound
a tenser *j* than the *j* in ***j**et*

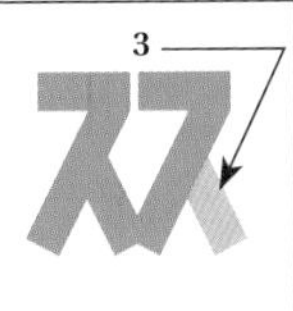

Romanized Letter	Hangeul	English sound
a	ㅏ	*ah* as in f***a***ther or b***a***rk
eo	ㅓ	*uh* as in f***u***n or s***o***n, with more rounded lips
o	ㅗ	*oh* as in l***o***w or t***oe***
u	ㅜ	*oo* as in bl***ue*** or t***oo***
eu	ㅡ	*eu* as in f***oo***t or p***u***t
i	ㅣ	*ee* as in s***ee*** or m***e***
ae	ㅐ	*eh* as in t***a***ke or ch***a***se
e	ㅔ	*eh* as in b***e***d or d***ea***d
wa	ㅘ	*wah* as in ***wi***se
wae	ㅙ	*weh* as in w***a***it or ***we***ight
oe	ㅚ	*weh* as in ***wa***it or ***we***ight
wo	ㅝ	*wo* as in ***wa***llet
we	ㅞ	*weh* as in ***wa***it or ***we***ight
wi	ㅟ	*we* as in ***wea***ve or ***wee***d
ui	ㅢ	a combination of *eu* and *i* above
ya	ㅑ	*ya* as in ***ya***rd
yeo	ㅕ	*yuh* as in ***you***ng
yo	ㅛ	*yo* as in ***yo***gurt (American pronunciation)
yu	ㅠ	*yoo* as in ***you***
yae	ㅒ	*yeh* as in ***ya***y

ye	ㅖ	*yeh* as in ***ya***y
g	ㄱ	a softer version (unvoiced) of g as in ***g***ood
n	ㄴ	*n* as in ***n***ame
d	ㄷ	a softer version (unvoiced) of *d* as in ***d***awn
r	ㄹ	a *r* that involves rolling and vibrating the tongue
m	ㅁ	m as in ***m***ask
b	ㅂ	a softer version (unvoiced) of *b* as in ***b***all
s	ㅅ	*s* as in ***s***ad
ng	ㅇ	n*g* as in so***ng*** (at the end of a word)
j	ㅈ	a softer version (unvoiced) of *j* as in ***j***et
ch	ㅊ	*ch* as in ***ch***art
k	ㅋ	*k* as in ***k***id
t	ㅌ	*t* as in ***t***all
p	ㅍ	*p* as in ***p***aper
h	ㅎ	*h* as in ***h***ow or ***h***ot
kk	ㄲ	a tenser *g* than the *g* in ***g***ood
tt	ㄸ	a tenser *d* than the *d* in ***d***og
pp	ㅃ	a tenser *b* than the *b* in ***b***all
ss	ㅆ	a tenser *s* than the *s* in ***s***ad
jj	ㅉ	a tenser *j* than the *j* in ***j***et

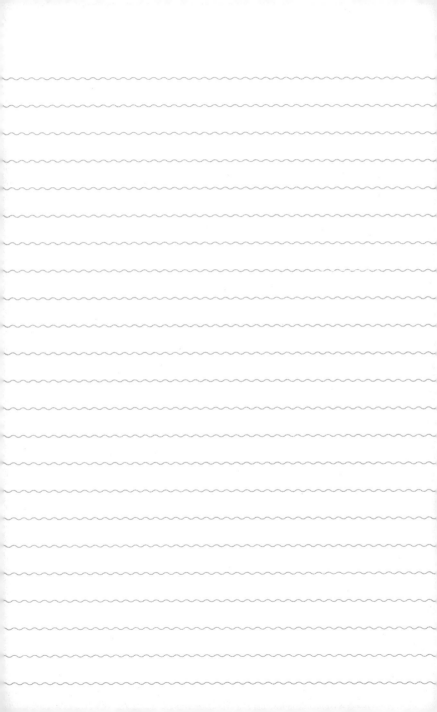

Chapter 04

How to Make a Hangeul Block

Creating a Hangeul block is like building with puzzle pieces using consonants and vowels!

Consonants are the sounds made with some closure or blockage of airflow in the mouth, like "b", "d", or "g".

Vowels are the sounds made with an open vocal tract, like "a", "e", or "o". We've practiced this before; now, by combining consonants and vowels, we can create these Hangeul blocks.

For example, consonants represent the building blocks of words, while vowels connect consonants and form syllables. By putting them together, we can form complete syllables and words in Hangeul.

Let's look at the different possible shapes these clusters can take. Remember, each one forms a syllable. In these images, C represents consonants, and V represents vowels.

Let's start with the most simple and common combinations: One consonant with one vowel.

ㄱ + ㅏ = 가

ㄴ + ㅏ = 나

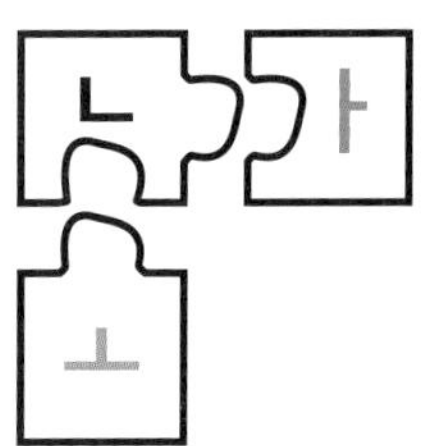

Do you still remember our Ganada Song?
Let's play some games!

Mini Quiz Can you try to fill out the missing words for our song!

가	__ㅏ	다	라	마	바	__ㅏ
__a	na	da	__a	ma	__a	sa
아	자	__ㅏ	카	__ㅏ	파	__ㅏ
a	ja	cha	__a	ta	pa	ha

아	야	어	여	오	요	우
a	ya	eo	yeo	o	yo	u
유	으	이				
yu	eu	i				

ANSWERS

g ㄴ r b ㅅ ㅊ k ㅌ ㅎ

Let's look at the Ganada song again. Can you identify and circle the combinations with just one consonant and one vowel?

가나다라마바사아자차카타파하
빠람빠람 Let's sing along

가나다라마바사아자차카타파하
빠람빠람 singing together

Let's walk and sing
Let's hold hands together
아야어여오요우유으이

가.슴을 펴고
나.를 따라해봐
다.함께
라.라라
마.음 열고
바.라봐
사.이좋게
아.름답게 Oh~
자.따라해봐
차.렷.하나둘셋
카.네이션
타.고서
파.란하늘
보고 웃어봐
하하하하
하!하!하!

가나다라마바사아자차카타파하
빠람빠람 Let's sing along

가나다라마바사아자차카타파하
빠람빠람 singing together

Let's walk and sing
Let's hold hands together
아야어여오요우유으이

We're together
Together is better
Me and You, we're one
Melodies are shared like a dream! Languages Our look, Oh!
All isn't the same / Many differences
Let's sing me and you / Melody makes us one, together!
Singing brings peace and love

가나다라마바사아자차카타파하
우리에게 꿈을 주는 글
가나다라마바사아자차카타파하
Born to give us hope and the dream

Let's walk and sing
Let's hold hands together
아야어여오요우유으이
Let's go !

C_1	V_2

These are syllable cluster shapes that put the vowel (i.e., side vowels) to the right side of the first consonant. The letters are sounded out in the order represented by the numbers in the boxes (1, 2, 3 etc.).

C_1	V_2
C_3	

C_1	V_2
C_3	C_4

다	Look at these examples of the combinations listed above.
달	닭

These are syllable cluster shapes that put the vowel underneath the first consonant (i.e.,bottom vowels). The letters are sounded out in the order represented by the numbers in the boxes.

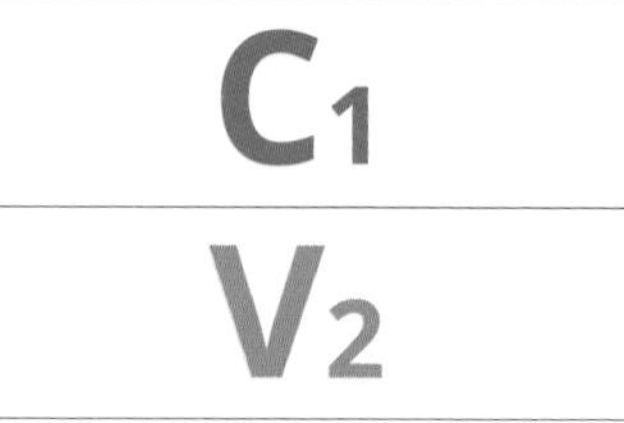

C1
V2
C3

C1	
V2	
C3	C4

Look at these examples of the combinations listed above.	모
목	몫

Let's look at the combination of consonants with vowels. The vowels ㅏ, ㅓ, and ㅣ attach to the side of the consonant, and the vowels ㅗ, ㅜ, and ㅡ attach to the bottom of the consonant. Make sure to look back at the romanization chart to check pronunciation!

Try to write the following words:

ㅏ

가지마 *Don't go* .... [gajima]

가족 *Family* .... [gajok]

ㅓ

저 *I* .... [jeo]

처음 *First time* .... [cheoeum]

ㅗ

노래 *Song* .... [norae]

조금 *A little* .... [jogeum]

ㅜ

누나 *Older sister* .... [nuna]

후루룩 *Slurping sound* .... [hurureuk]

ㅣ

다시 *Again* .... [dashi]

미소 *Smile* .... [miso]

ㄱ

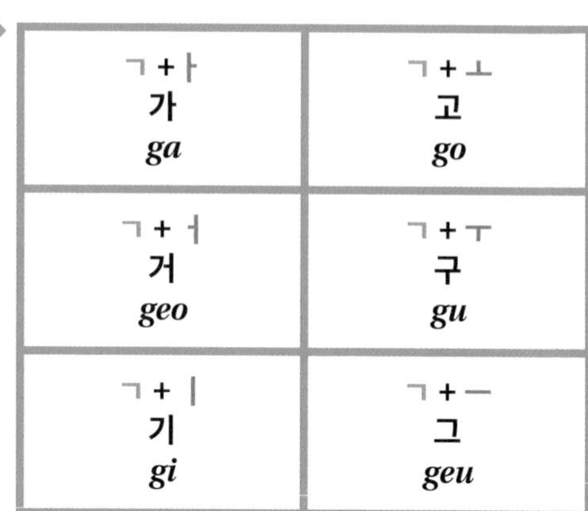

ㄱ + ㅏ **가** ***ga***	ㄱ + ㅗ **고** ***go***
ㄱ + ㅓ **거** ***geo***	ㄱ + ㅜ **구** ***gu***
ㄱ + ㅣ **기** ***gi***	ㄱ + ㅡ **그** ***geu***

Try to write the following words:

고기 *Meat* [gogi]

고	기						

가게 *Shop* [gage]

가	게						

기차 *Train* [gicha]

기	차						

ㄴ

ㄴ + ㅏ 나 *na*	ㄴ + ㅗ 노 *no*
ㄴ + ㅓ 너 *neo*	ㄴ + ㅜ 누 *nu*
ㄴ + ㅣ 니 *ni*	ㄴ + ㅡ 느 *neu*

Try to write the following words:

누나 *Older sister* [nuna]

누	나						

나이 *Age* [nai]

나	이						

노래 *Song* [norae]

노	래						

Fun Fact

In Korean, "**nuna**" is used by males to address an older sister or female, "**oppa**" by females for an older brother or male, "**eonni**" by females for an older sister or female, and "**hyung**" by males for an older brother or male.

ㄷ

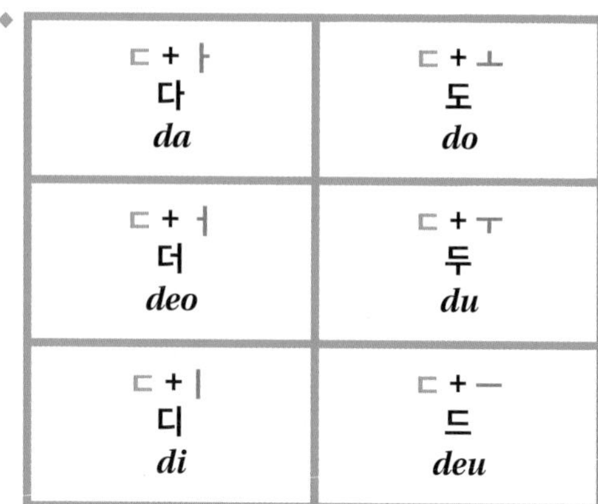

ㄷ + ㅏ 다 ***da***	ㄷ + ㅗ 도 ***do***
ㄷ + ㅓ 더 ***deo***	ㄷ + ㅜ 두 ***du***
ㄷ + ㅣ 디 ***di***	ㄷ + ㅡ 드 ***deu***

Try to write the following words:

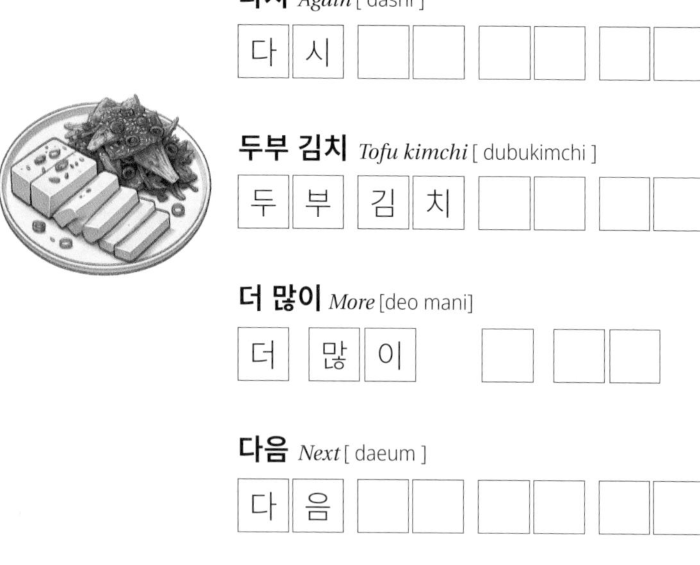

다시 *Again* [dashi]

다 시

두부 김치 *Tofu kimchi* [dubukimchi]

두 부 김 치

더 많이 *More* [deo mani]

더 많 이

다음 *Next* [daeum]

다 음

ㄹ

ㄹ + ㅏ 라 *ra*	ㄹ + ㅗ 로 *ro*
ㄹ + ㅓ 러 *reo*	ㄹ + ㅜ 루 *ru*
ㄹ + ㅣ 리 *ri*	ㄹ + ㅡ 르 *reu*

Try to write the following words:

라면 *Ramen* [ramyeon]

라	면						

리조트 *Resort* [rijoteu]

리	조	트			

로션 *Lotion* [rosyeon]

로	션						

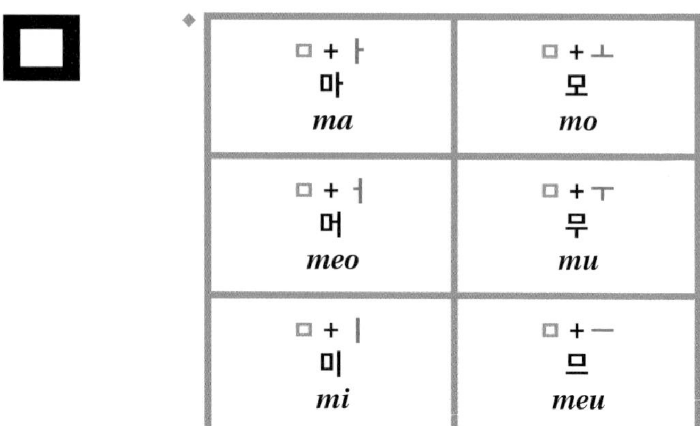

ㅁ

ㅁ + ㅏ 마 *ma*	ㅁ + ㅗ 모 *mo*
ㅁ + ㅓ 머 *meo*	ㅁ + ㅜ 무 *mu*
ㅁ + ㅣ 미 *mi*	ㅁ + ㅡ 므 *meu*

Try to write the following words:

마음 *Heart* [maeum]

마	음						

미소 *Smile* [miso]

미	소						

메뉴 *Menu* [menyu]

메	뉴						

ㅂ + ㅏ **바** ***ba***	ㅂ + ㅗ **보** ***bo***
ㅂ + ㅓ **버** ***beo***	ㅂ + ㅜ **부** ***bu***
ㅂ + ㅣ **비** ***bi***	ㅂ + ㅡ **브** ***beu***

Try to write the following words:

밥 *Rice* [bap]

밥

바다 *Sea* [bada]

바 다

비행기 *Airplane* [bihaenggi]

비 행 기

버스 *Bus* [beoseu]

버 스

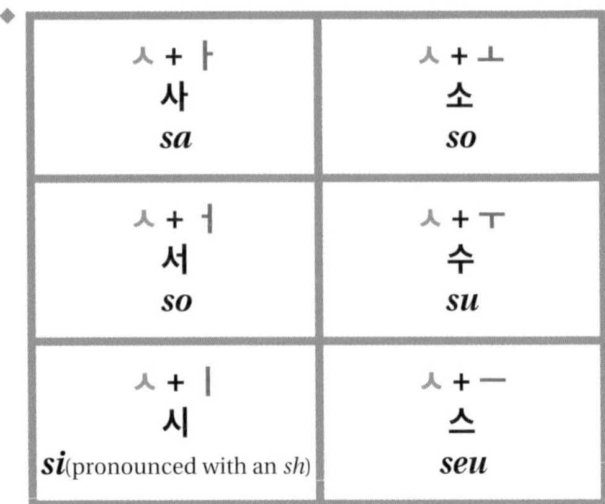

ㅅ + ㅏ 사 ***sa***	ㅅ + ㅗ 소 ***so***
ㅅ + ㅓ 서 ***so***	ㅅ + ㅜ 수 ***su***
ㅅ + ㅣ 시 ***si***(pronounced with an *sh*)	ㅅ + ㅡ 스 ***seu***

Try to write the following words:

사랑해 *I love you* [saranghae]

사 랑 해

수능 *Korean college entrance exam* [suneung]

수 능

소리 *Sound* [sori]

소 리

식당 *Restaurant* [sikdang]

식 당

Fun Fact

Suneung is Korea's national college entrance exam, similar to the SAT. It's crucial for university admission and influences students' futures significantly.

ㅇ + ㅏ 아 ***a***	ㅇ + ㅗ 오 ***o***
ㅇ + ㅓ 어 ***eo***	ㅇ + ㅜ 우 ***u***
ㅇ + ㅣ 이 ***i***	ㅇ + ㅡ 으 ***eu***

At the beginning of syllables, this consonant is silent.

Try to write the following words:

우리 *We/Us* [uri]

우	리						

아빠 *Dad* [appa]

아	빠						

영어 *English* [yeongeo]

영	어						

오늘 *Today* [oneul]

오	늘						

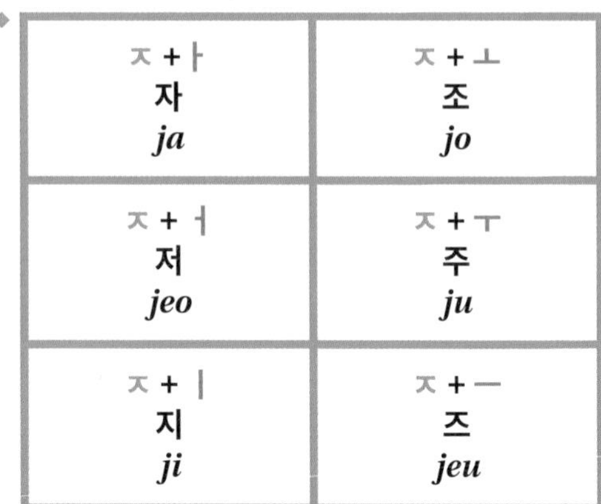

ㅈ + ㅏ 자 *ja*	ㅈ + ㅗ 조 *jo*
ㅈ + ㅓ 저 *jeo*	ㅈ + ㅜ 주 *ju*
ㅈ + ㅣ 지 *ji*	ㅈ + ㅡ 즈 *jeu*

Try to write the following words:

저 *I* [jeo]

저							

조금 *A little* [jogeum]

조	금						

잡채 *Japchae* [japchae]

잡	채						

지하철 *Subway* [jihacheol]

지	하	철			

The aspirated version of ㅈ

ㅊ + ㅏ 차 ***cha***	ㅊ + ㅗ 초 ***cho***
ㅊ + ㅓ 처 ***cheo***	ㅊ + ㅜ 추 ***chu***
ㅊ + ㅣ 치 ***chi***	ㅊ + ㅡ 츠 ***cheu***

Try to write the following words:

차 *Car* [cha]

차							

처음 *First time* [cheoeum]

처	음						

친구 *Friend* [chingu]

친	구						

초과 근무 *Overtime* [chogwa geunmu]

초	과	근	무				

Fun Fact

Overtime work is a significant issue in Korea. Many employees work long hours, often beyond their official workday, which can lead to stress, burnout, and work-life imbalance.

The aspirated version of ㄱ

ㅋ + ㅏ **카** ***ka***	ㅋ + ㅗ **코** ***ko***
ㅋ + ㅓ **커** ***keo***	ㅋ + ㅜ **쿠** ***ku***
ㅋ + ㅣ **키** ***ki***	ㅋ + ㅡ **크** ***keu***

Try to write the following words:

커피 *Coffee* [keopi]

커	피						

콜라 *Cola* [kolla]

콜	라						

코트 *Coat* [koteu]

코	트						

컴퓨터 *Computer* [keompyuteo]

컴	퓨	터			

The aspirated version of ㄷ

ㅌ + ㅏ 타 *ta*	ㅌ + ㅗ 토 *to*
ㅌ + ㅓ 터 *teo*	ㅌ + ㅜ 투 *tu*
ㅌ + ㅣ 티 *ti*	ㅌ + ㅡ 트 *teu*

Try to write the following words:

토마토 *Tomato* [tomato]

토	마	토			

티켓 *Ticket* [tiket]

티	켓						

택시 *Taxi* [taeksi]

택	시						

토너 *Toner* [toneo]

토	너						

The aspirated version of ㅂ

ㅍ + ㅏ 파 ***pa***	ㅍ + ㅗ 포 ***po***
ㅍ + ㅓ 퍼 ***peo***	ㅍ + ㅜ 푸 ***pu***
ㅍ + ㅣ 피 ***pi***	ㅍ + ㅡ 프 ***peu***

Try to write the following words:

파티 *Party* [pati]

파	티						

푸른 *Blue / Green* [pureun]

푸	른						

프라이머 *Primer* [peuraimeo]

프	라	이	머				

표 *Ticket* [pyo]

표							

Fun Fact

Pureun can describe both "blue" and "green". Historically, the language didn't differentiate between these two colors as distinctly as in English. Instead, 푸른 refers to a broad spectrum of cool colors that include both blue and green, especially when describing nature, like the sky or the grass.

ㅎ + ㅏ 하 ***ha***	ㅎ + ㅗ 호 ***ho***
ㅎ + ㅓ 허 ***heo***	ㅎ + ㅜ 후 ***hu***
ㅎ + ㅣ 히 ***hi***	ㅎ + ㅡ 흐 ***heu***

The aspirated version of ㅇ

Try to write the following words:

행복 *Happiness* [haengbok]

행	복						

하늘 *Sky* [haneul]

하	늘						

호텔 *Hotel* [hotel]

호	텔						

화장실 *Restroom* [hwajangsil]

화	장	실			

ㄲ

The reinforced version of ㄱ

ㄲ + ㅏ 까 ***kka***	ㄲ + ㅗ 꼬 ***kko***
ㄲ + ㅓ 꺼 ***kkeo***	ㄲ + ㅜ 꾸 ***kku***
ㄲ + ㅣ 끼 ***kki***	ㄲ + ㅡ 끄 ***kkeu***

Try to write the following words:

꼬마 *Kid* [kkoma]

꼬	마						

끄다 *To turn off* [kkeuda]

끄	다						

The reinforced version of ㄷ

ㄸ + ㅏ 따 *tta*	ㄸ + ㅗ 또 *tto*
ㄸ + ㅓ 떠 *tteo*	ㄸ + ㅜ 뚜 *ttu*
ㄸ + ㅣ 띠 *tti*	ㄸ + ㅡ 뜨 *tteu*

Try to write the following words:

또 *Again* [tto]

또							

뚜껑 *Lid* [ttukkeong]

뚜	껑						

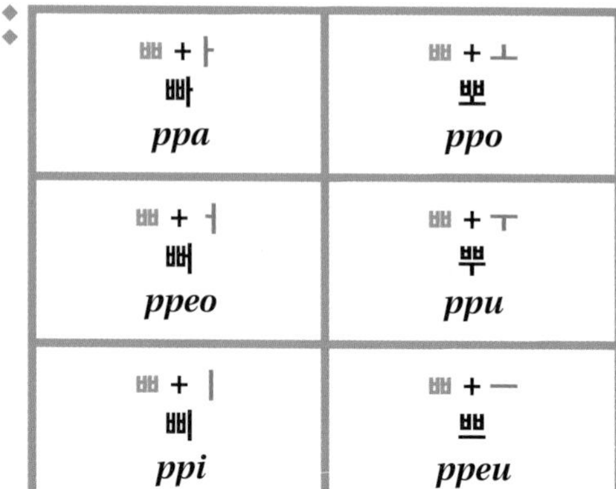

ㅃ + ㅏ 빠 ***ppa***	ㅃ + ㅗ 뽀 ***ppo***
ㅃ + ㅓ 뻐 ***ppeo***	ㅃ + ㅜ 뿌 ***ppu***
ㅃ + ㅣ 삐 ***ppi***	ㅃ + ㅡ 쁘 ***ppeu***

The reinforced version of ㅂ (p)

Try to write the following words:

뽀로로 *Pororo* [ppororo]

뽀 로 로

쁘띠 *Petite* [ppeutti]

쁘 띠

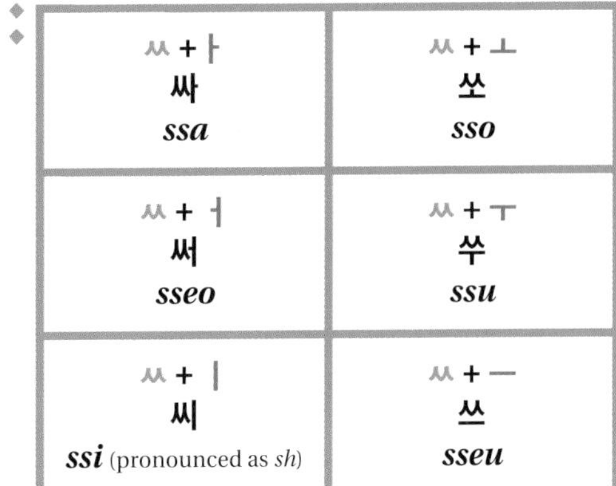

ㅆ + ㅏ **싸** ***ssa***	ㅆ + ㅗ **쏘** ***sso***
ㅆ + ㅓ **써** ***sseo***	ㅆ + ㅜ **쑤** ***ssu***
ㅆ + ㅣ **씨** ***ssi*** (pronounced as *sh*)	ㅆ + ㅡ **쓰** ***sseu***

The reinforced version of ㅅ

Try to write the following words:

싸가지 *Rude* [ssagaji]

싸	가	지			

쓰다 *To write/use* [sseuda]

쓰	다						

ㅉ + ㅏ 짜 *jja*	ㅉ + ㅗ 쪼 *jjo*
ㅉ + ㅓ 쩌 *jjeo*	ㅉ + ㅜ 쭈 *jju*
ㅉ + ㅣ 찌 *jji*	ㅉ + ㅡ 쯔 *jjeu*

The reinforced version of ㅈ

Try to write the following words:

짜장면 *Jjajangmyeon* [jjajangmyeon]

짜	장	면			

짬뽕 *Jjamppong* [jjamppong]

짬	뽕						

Chapter 05

Consonants at the Bottom

[Batchim]

CONSONANTS AT THE END OF SYLLABLES

When the consonant comes at the end of the syllable, it always sits at the bottom, whether the vowel is a "side" vowel or a "bottom" vowel. The consonant sound at the end of the syllable is different from the consonant sound at the beginning of the syllable. The following are examples of each consonant at the end of a syllable.

At the end of a syllable, ㄱ makes a soft *k* sound by closing up the throat, as in loc***k*** or ca***k***e.

약 [yak] **medicine**
죽 [juk] **porridge**

Try to write the following words:

식당 *Restaurant* [sikdang]

....

음악 *Music* [eumak]

....

한국 *Korea* [hanguk]

....

At the end of a syllable, ㄴ makes an *n* sound, as in ru***n*** or ma***n***. It is the same sound as when it appears in the beginning.

선	[seon]	**line**
분	[bun]	**person**

Try to write the following words:

은행 *Bank* [eunhaeng]

....

사진 *Photo* [sajin]

....

신분증 *ID Card* [sinbunjeung]

....

관광지 *Tourist attraction* [gwangwangji]

....

At the end of a syllable, ㄷ makes a soft *t* sound by closing up the throat, as in ha***t*** or ho***t***.

받	[bat]	**to receive (받다 *batda*)**
곧	[got]	**soon**

Try to write the following words:

받다 *Receive* [batda]

믿다 *Believe* [mitda]

At the end of a syllable, ㄹ makes an *l* sound, as in ha***ll*** or sma***ll***.

털	[teol]	**fur**
굴	[gul]	**cave**

Try to write the following words:

월요일 *Monday* [woryoil]

호텔 *Hotel* [hotel]

불고기 *Grilled meat* [bulgogi]

서울 *Seoul* [seoul]

갈비탕 *Beef rib soup* [galbitang]

At the end of a syllable, ㅁ makes an *m* sound, as in hi***m*** or ja***m***. It is the same sound as when it appears in the beginning.

잠	[jam]	**sleep**
봄	[bom]	**spring**

Try to write the following words:

감자탕 *Pork bone soup* [gamjatang]

....

짐 *Luggage* [jim]

....

음식 *Food* [eumsik]

....

At the end of a syllable, ㅂ makes a soft *p* sound by closing up the throat, as in sla***p*** or to***p***.

집 [jip] **house**

즙 [jeup] **juice**

Try to write the following words:

김밥 *Seaweed rice rolls* [gimbap]

잡채 *Stir-fried glass noodles* [japchae]

밥 *Rice* [bap]

At the end of a syllable, ㅅ makes a soft *t* sound by closing up the throat , as in ha***t*** or ho***t***.

것	[geot]	**thing**
곳	[got]	**place**

Try to write the following words:

맛 *Taste* [mat]

옷 *Clothes* [ot]

낫 *Sickle* [nat]

At the end of a syllable, ㅇ makes an *ng* sound, as in so***ng*** or thi***ng***.

방 [bang] **room**

등 [deung] **lantern, light**

Try to write the following words:

공항 *Airport* [gonghang]

....

중앙 *Center* [jungang]

....

성공 *Success* [seonggong]

....

영어 *English* [yeongeo]

....

At the end of a syllable, ㅈ makes a soft *t* sound by closing up the throat, as in ha***t*** or ho***t***.

낮	[nat]	**afternoon**
늦	[got]	**late (늦다 *neutda*)**

Try to write the following words:

맞아! *Correct!* [maja]

곶감 *Persimmon* [gotgam]

At the end of a syllable, ㅊ makes a soft *t* sound by closing up the throat, as in ha***t*** or ho***t***.

빛 [bit] **light**

꽃 [ggot] **kkot**

Try to write the following words:

윷놀이 *A traditional board game* [yutnori]

....

꽃병 *Vase* [kkotbyeong]

....

Fun Fact

Yutnori is a traditional Korean board game played with four wooden sticks called 윷 (yut). Players or teams throw the sticks to move markers around a board, aiming to complete a circuit before the opponent. It's popular during holidays like Lunar New Year.

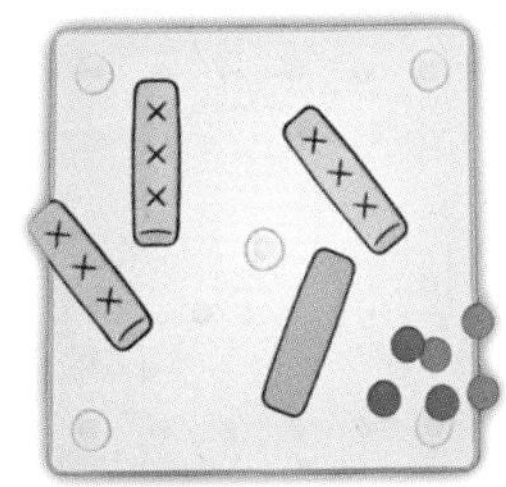

At the end of a syllable, ㅋ makes a soft *k* sound by closing up the throat, as in loc***k*** or ca***k***e.

엌	[eok]	**kitchen (부엌 *bueok*)**
읔	[euk]	**the ㅋ letter (키읔 *kieuk*)**

Try to write the following words:

부엌 *kitchen* [bueok]

At the end of a syllable, ㅌ makes a soft *t* sound, as in hat or hot. You won't actually pronounce the t—rather let your tongue stop before letting the *t* sound out. Take a look at the following two examples:

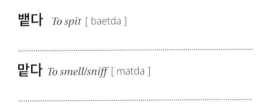

밑	[mit]	**underneath**
붙	[but]	**to attach (붙다 *butda*)**

Try to write the following words:

뱉다 *To spit* [baetda]

....

맡다 *To smell/sniff* [matda]

....

At the end of a syllable, ㅍ makes a *p* sound by closing up the throat, as in sla***p*** or to***p***.

잎	[ip]	**leaf**
높	[nop]	**high (높다 *nopda*)**

Try to write the following words:

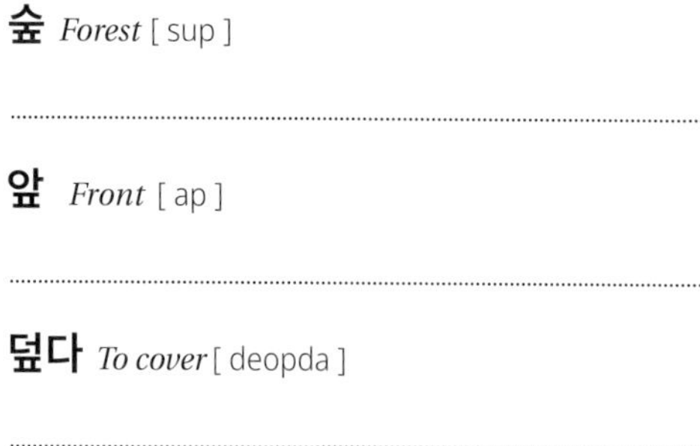

숲 *Forest* [sup]

앞 *Front* [ap]

덮다 *To cover* [deopda]

At the end of a syllable, ㅎ makes a soft aspirated *t* sound, as in ha***t*** or ho***t*** with some puffs of air.

닿	[nat]	**to touch (닿다 *data*)**
놓	[not]	**to put/set (something) down (놓다 *nota*)**

Try to write the following words:

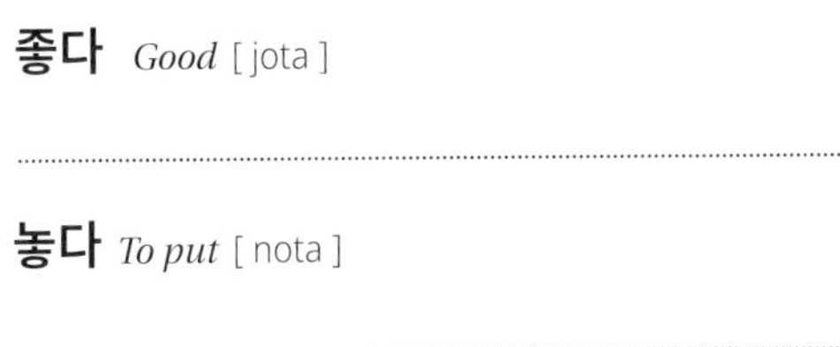

At the end of a syllable, ㄲ makes a soft *k* sound by closing up the throat, as in loc***k*** or ca***k***e.

닦	[dakk]	**to wipe clean (닦다 *dakkda*)**
묶	[mukk]	**to tie (묶다 *mukkda*)**

Try to write the following words:

밖에 *Outside* [bakke]

At the end of a syllable, ㅆ makes a soft *t* sound by closing up the throat, as in ha***t*** or ho***t***.

었 [et] **commonly found in past tense**

ㅆ doesn't usually appear as a final letter with ㅗ, ㅜ, or ㅡ vowels.
ㄸ, ㅃ, and ㅉ don't usually appear at the end of a syllable.

Try to write the following words:

있다 *To exist* [itda]

....

맛있다 *Delicious* [masitda]

....

Consonant clusters often appear at the end of Korean words, following the batchim pronunciation rules. These clusters simplify into seven core sounds: ㄱ, ㄴ, ㄷ, ㄹ, ㅁ, ㅂ, and ㅇ, especially before another consonant or at the word's end. The table below shows examples of how these clusters are simplified.

WORD	ROMANIZATION	PRONOUNCE
닭	dalk	*dak*
밟	balp	*bap*
읽	ilk	*ik*
붉	bulk	*buk*
꿇	ggult	*ggul*
값	gapt	*gap*
옳	olt	*ol*
얹	eont	*eon*
읊	eulp	*eup*

What is the name of your favourite K-pop band?

....

What is the name of your favourite K-pop song?

....

What is the name of your BIAS?

....

Now, pick your favourite K-pop song or any Korean song. Can you try to find more words that have double consonants at the bottom? Write them down here:

Chapter 06

Putting It All Together

Many words in Korean are formed by putting together multiple syllables. Sometimes, the ending of one syllable will affect the pronunciation at the beginning of the next syllable. The following are examples of some of these syllable combinations.

Sound Change Rule 1

When one syllable is following by another syllable that begins with the silent consonant ㅇ, the sound from the first syllable carries over. Look at the example:

먹어요 to eat ➡ 머거요 *meo**g**eoyo*

받아요 to receive ➡ 바다요 *ba**d**ayo*

달아요 to be sweet ➡ 다라요 *da**r**ayo*

The spelling doesn't change–but the pronunciation does!

Try to pronounce these words!

읽어요 To read ···▸ [일거요] *ilgeoyo*

앉아요 To sit ···▸ [안자요] *anjayo*

좋아요 To be good ···▸ [조아요] *joayo*

Sound Change Rule 2

Some letters change pronunciation when followed or preceded by a nasal consonant (ㄴ, ㅁ, ㅇ). Look at the following examples to find patterns:

합니다 to do	➡	함니다 *hamnida*
국물 broth	➡	궁물 *gungmul*
정리 arrangement	➡	정니 *jeongni*
ㅂ + ㄴ/ㅁ/ㅇ	➡	ㅁ + ㄴ/ㅁ/ㅇ
ㄱ + ㄴ/ㅁ/ㅇ	➡	ㅇ + ㄴ/ㅁ/ㅇ
ㄴ/ㅁ/ㅇ + ㄹ	➡	ㄴ/ㅁ/ㅇ + ㄴ

There are more examples of this rule, so keep a look out!

Try to pronounce these words!

독립 Independence	··· ▸	[동닙] *dongnip*
박물관 Museum	··· ▸	[방물관] *bangmulgwan*
작년 Last year	··· ▸	[장년] *jangnyeon*

Sound Change Rule 3

When two ㄹ characters appear next to each other, they make an l sound. When ㄴ appears next to ㄹ, ㄴ also changes to ㄹ. Look at the following examples:

연락 contact through message or call

➡ 열락 *yeollak*

전라도 Jeolla Province

➡ 절라도 *jeollado*

난로 stove ➡ 날로 *nallo*

ㄹ + ㄹ ➡ ㄹ + ㄹ

ㄴ + ㄹ ➡ ㄹ + ㄹ

Remember that only the pronunciation, not the spelling, changes!

Try to pronounce these words!

설날 Lunar New Year

···› [설랄] *seollal*

신라 Name of an ancient Korean kingdom

···› [실라] *silla*

한라산 Name of a famous mountain in Korea

···› [할라산] *hallasan*

Fun Fact

Seollal is the Korean Lunar New Year, a major holiday celebrating the first day of the lunar calendar. Families gather to perform ancestral rites, eat traditional foods like tteokguk (rice cake soup), and play games like 윷놀이. It's a time for honoring ancestors and spending time with family.

Sound Change Rule 4

When ㄷ or ㅌ is followed by 이 or 히, they change to ㅈ or ㅊ respectively. Look at the following examples:

맏이 eldest child ➡ 마지 *maji*

닫혀요 to be closed ➡ 다쳐요 *dachyeoyo*

같이 together ➡ 가치 *gachi*

ㄷ + ㅇ ➡ ㅈ

ㄷ + ㅎ ➡ ㅊ

ㅌ + ㅇ/ㅎ ➡ ㅊ

While the pronunciation changes, the spelling remains the same.

Try to pronounce these words!

굳이 Insistently ···› [구지] *guji*

갇히다 To be locked up ···› [가치다] *gachida*

밭이 Field ···› [바치] *bachi*

LET'S TRY TO READ SOME COMMON WORDS!

사람	*Person*	집	*House*
물	*Water*	밥	*Rice / Meal*
책	*Book*	차	*Car / Tea*
나무	*Tree*	고양이	*Cat*
개	*Dog*	꽃	*Flower*
문	*Door*	공	*Ball*
손	*Hand*	눈	*Eye / Snow*
산	*Mountain*	시간	*Time*
하늘	*Sky*	얼굴	*Face*

K-FOOD CHALLENGE

Take 30 seconds to think about your top 3 K-food. Draw them on the space provided. Then, look for how they are written in Korean!

Chapter 07

Essential Korean Expressions and Fun K-Words

안녕하세요	Hello
반갑습니다	Nice to meet you
안녕히 계세요	Goodbye [you're leaving]
저는 [NAME] 입니다	My name is ____
감사합니다	Thank you
괜찮아요	It's fine/No problem
잠시만요	Excuse me [getting someone's attention]
네	Yes
아니요	No
미안해요	Sorry
어디에서 오셨어요?	Where are you from?
영어 할 수 있으세요?	Do you speak English?
이해가 되지 않아요	I don't understand
[NOUN] 있어요?	Is there ____?/Do you have ____?

[NOUN] 어디예요?	Where is ____?
이게 뭐예요?	What is this?
얼마예요?	How much is it?
이거 주세요	Please can I have this/I want this
도와주세요	Please help me
잘 먹겠습니다	Thank you for the meal [before eating]
잘 먹었습니다	Thank you for the meal [after eating]
맛있어요	It's delicious
카드로 지불해도 될까요?	Can I pay by card?
봉투를 주시겠어요?	Can I get a bag?
너무 비쌉니다	It's too expensive

K-POP WORDS

앨범 *Album*

빌보드 *Billboard*

보이그룹 *Boy group*

안무 *Choreography*

컴백 *Comeback*

작곡가 *Composer*

콘서트 *Concert*

댄스팀 *Dance team*

데뷔 *Debut*

눈 *Eyes*

팬 *Fan*

팬덤 *Fandom*

팬미팅 *Fan meeting*

이별 *Farewell/Breakup*

걸그룹 *Girl group*

손 *Hand*

행복 *Happiness*

가슴 *Heart/Chest*

마음 *Heart/Mind*

나 *I/Me*

아이돌 *Idol*

그룹 *K-pop group*

리더 *Leader*

레전드 *Legend*

그리움 *Longing/Nostalgia*

사랑 *Love*

메인보컬 *Main vocal*

멤버 *Member*

기억 *Memory*

뮤비 *MV*

뮤비촬영 *MV shooting*

이제 *Now*

오에스티 *Original soundtrack*

공연 *Performance*

연습실 *Practice room*

홍보 *Promotion*

랩 *Rap*

랩라인 *Rap line*

가수 *Singer*

K-POP WORDS

미소 *Smile*

노래 *Song*

소리 *Sound*

목소리 *Voice*

무대 *Stage*

서브보컬 *Sub vocal*

눈물 *Tears*

그때 *Then/At that time*

시간 *Time*

연습생 *Trainee*

트레이너 *Trainer*

함께 *Together*

예능 *Variety show*

보컬 *Vocal*

브이로그 *Vlog*

기다림 *Waiting*

너 *You*

그대 *You (formal)*

K-BEAUTY WORDS

액세서리 *Accessory*

미용 *Beauty*

브랜드 *Brand*

캐주얼 *Casual*

클렌징 *Cleansing*

의상 *Clothing*

컬렉션 *Collection*

코디 *Coordination*

화장품 *Cosmetics*

뷰티크리에이터 *Beauty creator*

블러셔 *Blusher*

디자이너 *Designer*

드레스 *Dress*

아이라이너 *Eyeliner*

패션 *Fashion*

의상디자인 *Fashion design*

패션아이콘 *Fashion icon*

패션쇼 *Fashion show*

포멀 *Formal*

파운데이션 *Foundation*

헤어컷 *Haircut*

립스틱 *Lipstick*

로션 *Lotion*

명품 *Luxury*

메이크업 *Makeup*

마스카라 *Mascara*

모델 *Model*

수분크림 *Moisturizer*

미용실 *Salon*

세럼 *Serum*

셔츠 *Shirt*

쇼핑 *Shopping*

피부관리 *Skin care*

스타일 *Style*

스타일링 *Styling*

스타일리스트 *Stylist*

트렌드 *Trend*

토너 *Toner*

K-TRAVEL

숙소 *Accommodation*

비행기 *Airplane*

공항 *Airport*

북촌한옥마을 *Bukchon Hanok Village*

버스 *Bus*

창덕궁 *Changdeokgung Palace*

경복궁 *Gyeongbokgung Palace*

한강공원 *Hangang Park*

호텔 *Hotel*

인사동 *Insadong*

제주도 *Jeju Island*

여행가방 *Luggage*

지도 *Map*

남산서울타워 *Namsan Seoul Tower*

여권 *Passport*

비행기표 *Plane ticket*

렌터카 *Rental car*

예약 *Reservation*

관광객 *Tourist*

관광명소 *Tourist attraction*

여행 *Travel*

여행사 *Travel agency*

여행일정 *Travel itinerary*

기차 *Train*

관광 *Sightseeing*

지하철 *Subway*

비자 *Visa*

K-DRAMA WORDS

액션 *Action*

배우 *Actor*

여배우 *Actress*

연기 *Acting*

오디션 *Audition*

방송 *Broadcast*

방송국 *Broadcasting Station*

캐릭터 *Character*

코미디 *Comedy*

드라마 *Drama*

감독 *Director*

촬영 *Filming*

주인공 *Main character*

멜로 *Melodrama*

프로듀서 *Producer*

리메이크 *Remake*

로맨스 *Romance*

시즌 *Season*

대본 *Script*

조연 *Supporting role*

K-WORK

상사 *Boss*

경력 *Career*

회사 *Company*

출근 *Commute*

동료 *Colleague*

직원 *Employee*

직업 *Job*

퇴근 *Leave the office*

회의 *Meeting*

신입사원 *New employee*

프로젝트 *Project*

승진 *Promotion*

채용 *Recruitment*

월급 *Salary*

업무 *Task*

팀워크 *Teamwork*

휴가 *Vacation*

일 *Work*

근무시간 *Working hours*

직장 *Workplace*

K-FOOD

비빔밥 *Bibimbap (mixed rice with vegetables and meat)*

소고기 *Beef*

불고기 *Bulgogi (marinated beef)*

닭고기 *Chicken*

냉면 *Cold noodles*

생선 *Fish*

음식 *Food*

과일 *Fruit*

김밥 *Gimbap (Korean rice roll)*

김치 *Kimchi*

고기 *Meat*

돼지고기 *Pork*

밥 *Rice/Meal*

떡 *Rice cake*

해산물 *Seafood*

반찬 *Side dishes*

국 *Soup*

간장 *Soy sauce*

찌개 *Stew*

야채 *Vegetables*

Congratulations!
You've learned Hangeul!

You've reached the end of your **Annyeong? Hangeul!** journey.

From mastering the basic consonants and vowels to forming your very first words, you've taken big steps in learning the Korean language. We hope you had as much fun learning and practicing as we did guiding you through each step of the journey.

But remember, this is just the beginning! There's a whole world of Korean language and culture waiting for you to explore.

In the next book, we'll dive deeper into Korean grammar, expressions, and more exciting language tips.

Thank you for joining us on this adventure. We can't wait to see you in the next book, where we'll continue this amazing journey together.

Until then, 안녕히 계세요!

Shall we start practicing Hangeul now?

안녕? 한글!

초판인쇄 2024년 10월 09일
초판발행 2024년 10월 09일

지은이 조지은, 데릭 드릭스, 김형석
펴낸이 허대우

마케팅 박상호
편집 및 디자인 브런치파크
표지 이미지 이정진
캐릭터 디자인 이채민

펴낸곳 주식회사 헬로우코리안
주소 경기도 고양시 덕양구 향동로 217, 10층 KA1014호
문의 hello@hellokorean.co.kr
출판신고 2024년 6월 28일 제395-2024-000141호
인쇄 헬로우프린텍

ISBN 979-11-988638-0-5 93700
eBook ISBN 979-11-988638-1-2 15700